The
NAMES
of
JESUS

Other titles by Warren W. Wiersbe (selected)

The NAMES — *of* — JESUS

Warren W. Wiersbe

Baker Books
A Division of Baker Book House Co
Grand Rapids, Michigan 49516

© 1997 by Warren W. Wiersbe

Published by Baker Books
a division of Baker Book House Company
P.O. Box 6287, Grand Rapids, MI 49516–6287

Printed in the United States of America

Library of Congress Cataloging-in-Publication Data is on file at the Library of Congress, Washington, D.C.

For information about academic books, resources for Christian leaders, and all new releases available from Baker Book House, visit our web site:
http://www.bakerbooks.com

All scripture quotations are from NKJV unless indicated otherwise.

CONTENTS

CONTENTS

PREFACE

The five studies in the first section of the book were originally published by Tyndale House in the book *His Name Is Wonderful*. The book is now out of print; but over the years I received so many expressions of appreciation for these studies that I thought it wise to include them. After all, they deal with five of the most important names of our Lord.

The studies in the second section were originally given as radio messages over Back to the Bible Broadcast, and were published in the booklet *The Wonderful Names of Jesus*. I have revised and expanded them for this book. However, I have retained the informal style of the radio messages.

May his name ever be glorified!

Warren W. Wiersbe

INTRODUCTION

"What's in a name?"

Juliet asked Romeo that question in Shakespeare's famous play and then answered it herself: "What's in a name? That which we call a rose, by any other word would smell as sweet."

Granted, fair Juliet. But you and I and Romeo are people, not plants, and we know what our names are. Names must make a difference; otherwise, why would some people go to court to have their names changed? And why do many parents struggle over choosing names for their children? At some point in our childhood, many of us complained about the names our parents gave us and perhaps were grateful when somebody pinned a nickname on us. Sometimes joking about a fellow's name could be a declaration of war. Names do make a difference—if not to roses, at least to people.

Names are especially meaningful when you move into the Bible world. God named the first man "Adam," because he was made from the dust of the ground (Gen. 1:26–27). (In Hebrew, "Adam" means "earth.") God changed Abram's name to "Abraham," which means "the father of many nations" (Gen. 17:5–8), a perfect description of the patriarch. When God told the aged Abraham and Sarah they were going to have a son, they laughed; so their son was named "Isaac," which means "laughter" (Gen. 17:19; 21:1–7). That's a much happier choice than the one Rachel made when she named her boy "Ben-o-ni" which means "son of my sorrow" (Gen. 35:16–20). Of course, she was dying when she chose the name; but "son of my sorrow" is still a terrible weight to hang on any boy. Imagine going through life with a name that reminded you (and your friends) that your birth may have caused your mother's death! Jacob wisely changed the name to "Benjamin," which means "son of my right hand."

Jesus changed Simon's name to "Peter," which means "a rock" (John 1:40–42). At the time, the big fisherman may have looked more like shifting sand; but Jesus saw the potential that was there and helped him to live up to his new name.

Yes, names make a difference in the world of the Bible, and the most important names are those associated with our Savior. "You shall call His name JESUS, for He will save His people from their sins" (Matt. 1:21). "Jesus" is the Greek form of the Hebrew name "Joshua"; and both of them mean "the Lord is salvation." There are hundreds of names and titles of Jesus Christ in the Bible, and each one is a dual revelation to us. It reveals what Jesus Christ is in himself, as well as what he wants to do for us. Each name that he bears indicates some blessing that he shares, and we can appropriate these blessings by faith.

Seven hundred years before Jesus was born, the prophet Isaiah saw his coming. His record is in Isaiah 9:6: "For unto us a Child is born, unto us a Son is given; and the government shall be upon His shoulder. And His name shall be called Wonderful, Counselor, Mighty God, Everlasting Father, Prince of Peace."

Isaiah saw that this child was unique, for he was "born" and he was "given." In other words, this child was both God and man! As man, he was *born* and shared in our human nature, though sinless. As God, he was *given*—the Father's love gift to a sinful world. This child was God in human flesh!

What would this child do? He would grow up and one day take the government of mankind upon his shoulder and bring order and peace to a world filled with confusion and war. But before taking the government upon his shoulder, he would take a cross upon his shoulder, and then die upon that cross, bearing in his body the sins of the world. Before he could wear the diadem of glory as King of Kings, he had to wear a shameful crown of thorns and give his life as a sacrifice for the sins of the world. The kingly Lion of the tribe of Judah first had to come as the lowly Lamb of God; for until the debt of sin had been paid, God's righteous government could not be established.

In Isaiah 9:6, there's but a little space between the word "given" and the phrase "and the government"; but so far, that little space represents over nineteen centuries of history. Jesus Christ finished his work on earth and then returned to heaven, promising that he would come again. One day he shall return to this earth and take the government upon his shoulder. Isaiah saw that event, too. Ponder these promises:

> Of the increase of His government and peace there will be no end, upon the throne of David, and over His kingdom, to order it and establish it with judgment and justice from that time forward, even forever. The zeal of the LORD of hosts will perform this. (9:7)
> But with righteousness shall He judge the poor. . . . The wolf also shall dwell with the lamb, and the leopard shall

lie down with the young goat; and the calf and the young lion and the fatling together; and a little child shall lead them. . . . They shall not hurt nor destroy in all My holy mountain: for the earth shall be full of the knowledge of the LORD, as the waters cover the sea. (11:4, 6, 9)

Then the eyes of the blind shall be opened, and the ears of the deaf shall be unstopped. Then the lame shall leap like a deer, and the tongue of the dumb sing. For waters shall burst forth in the wilderness, and streams in the desert. . . . And the ransomed of the LORD shall return, and come to Zion with singing, with everlasting joy on their heads. They shall obtain joy and gladness, and sorrow and sighing shall flee away. (35:5–6, 10).

What a marvelous planet this will be when Jesus Christ returns to take the government upon his shoulder! But must we wait until then before we can enjoy his reign? No! You and I can turn the government of our lives over to him today! And when we do, all that is expressed in his names will become real in our own daily experience—"Wonderful, Counselor, Mighty God, Everlasting Father, Prince of Peace."

His name is *Wonderful:* this takes care of the *dullness of life.* No longer must we live on the cheap substitutes of the world in order to have excitement and enjoyment. Jesus Christ makes *everything* wonderful because Wonderful is his name.

His name is *Counselor:* this takes care of the *decisions of life.* The problems of life need perplex and paralyze us no longer, wondering what step to take next. With Jesus Christ as our Counselor, we have the wisdom we need to make the right decisions.

His name is *Mighty God:* this takes care of the *demands of life.* And life *is* demanding! Sometimes we feel like giving up and running off to hide somewhere; but through

Jesus Christ, we can face life courageously and have the strength we need to stay on the job and conquer.

His name is *Everlasting Father:* this takes care of the *dimensions of life.* What we are and what we do is part of eternity! A whole new dimension of living is ours through Jesus Christ, when the government of life is on his shoulder.

His name is *Prince of Peace:* this takes care of the *disturbances of life.* In the storms of life, how we long for peace within! What we wouldn't give to have poise and confidence in a threatening world! The answer is Jesus Christ, the Prince of Peace. When he controls the government of your life, he gives you a peace that passes all understanding and explanation.

It's a mistake to profess to trust Jesus Christ to save us and then go on living the way we please. Either the profession is false or we have a faulty understanding of who Jesus is. We must surrender our all to him and let him be the Lord of our lives. We must, by faith, place the government of our lives upon his shoulder.

For you, individually, it means surrendering your body to him as "a living sacrifice" (Rom. 12:1), so that he can walk in your body and work through your body to accomplish his purposes on earth. It also means yielding your mind and learning his truth from his Word: "And do not be conformed to this world, but be transformed by the renewing of your mind. . . ." (Rom. 12:2a).

It also means giving Christ your will: "that you may prove what is that good and acceptable and perfect will of God" (Rom. 12:2b). Finally, it means giving him your heart, your love. "If you love Me, keep My commandments" (John 14:15). When he has your body, mind, will, and heart, then he can reign in your life because the government will be on his shoulder.

As Jesus reigns in your life, you start to "reign in life through the One, Jesus Christ" (Rom. 5:17). Jesus doesn't ask you to abdicate the throne, for then you would become a mere puppet, without personality or the ability to act. All he asks is that you allow him to share the throne with you so that together you face life's challenges, solve life's problems, and accomplish life's purposes. Jesus doesn't do it *instead of you,* as though you were a lifeless robot; nor does he do it *in spite of you,* as though what you did made little difference. Rather, he does it in you and through you as you worship, pray, meditate on the Word, and obey him through the power of the Spirit.

If you have never taken this step before, just now, by faith, put the government of your life in his hands and on his shoulder. Tell Jesus that you want to "reign in life," no matter what the cost might be.

PART 1

The Names of Jesus from Isaiah 9:6

WONDERFUL

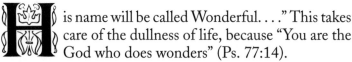

His name will be called Wonderful. . . ." This takes care of the dullness of life, because "You are the God who does wonders" (Ps. 77:14).

Bertrand Russell claimed that "at least half the sins of mankind" were caused by the fear of boredom. Perhaps this explains why children don't usually commit the kinds of sins that their elders commit, since, for the most part, children live in a world filled with wonder. A child can stare at a butterfly perched on a flower or at fish swimming in a pool and be perfectly content. Jesus may have had this in mind when he warned a group of adults, "Unless you are converted and become as little children, you will by no means enter the kingdom of heaven" (Matt. 18:3).

In today's society, we're surrounded by the miracles of modern science; yet people are bored, some of them to such an extent that they take their own lives. We face a population explosion; yet millions of people are slowly dying of the effects of loneliness and boredom. Our cities are crowded; yet hearts are empty. Henry David Thoreau once described the city as "hundreds of people being lonely together." In a world filled with exciting, electronic marvels, you would think that life would be exciting. However, for many people, life is just plain dull. They look for new toys, but once the novelty has worn off they go back to the same old routine. Obviously, something is wrong.

Wonder versus Novelty

Let's start with the basic question: What is wonder? Many different concepts cluster around the word "wonder": amazement, surprise, astonishment, awe, admiration, perhaps even bewilderment, and even worship. The Hebrew word that Isaiah used means "to separate, to distinguish." Throughout the Old Testament, it is translated a number of interesting ways: marvelous, hidden, too high, too difficult, miracle. It carries the basic meaning of being unique and different.

But we must be careful to distinguish "wonder" from some of the substitute ideas that might lead us astray. True wonder has depth. It isn't a shallow emotion or a passing wave of excitement. Wonder penetrates; it goes much deeper than the exciting or the sensational. The reason is that wonder has value; it isn't cheap amusement. When a person experiences true wonder, it enriches him and leaves him a better person. True wonder will draw the very best out of us and put the very best into us. True wonder creates in us an attitude of humility: we're overwhelmed and sense in ourselves the greatness of God and the littleness of man. David knew this feeling when he said, "When I consider Your heavens, the work of Your fingers, the moon and the stars, which You have ordained; what is man that

You art mindful of him, and the son of man, that You visit him?" (Ps. 8:3–4).

Many people have the false notion that wonder is based on ignorance. "Bring an ignorant savage to the big city," they say, "and he'll be amazed at everything he sees." But true wonder is based on knowledge, not ignorance. The more we know, the more we wonder. This childlike spirit of wonder isn't founded on innocent ignorance; it's founded on an inquisitive and intelligent attitude toward reality.

Wise people gladly confess how little they really know. Each trickle of truth only leads to a river that takes us to the vast ocean of knowledge whose depths we can't measure. Excitement over novelty passes once the novelty is explained and understood; wonder grows deeper when knowledge increases. British mathematician and scientist Sir Isaac Newton wrote: "To myself I seem to have been only like a boy playing on the seashore and diverting myself in now and then finding a smoother pebble or a prettier shell than ordinary, whilst the great ocean of truth lay all undiscovered before me." Albert Einstein put it this way: "The fairest thing we can experience is the mysterious. . . . He who knows it not, can no longer wonder, no longer feel amazement, is as good as dead, a snuffed out candle."

Finally, true wonder possesses the whole person, the mind the heart, the will. Wonder isn't an isolated experience that perplexes the mind or stirs the emotions. True wonder captures the whole person; otherwise the experience is simply novelty or surprise, merely a passing entertainment. This is because true wonder is an attitude of life and not an interruption or an isolated event. The person who lives in childlike wonder always lives this way. Wonder isn't something we turn on and off like a radio; true wonder is the total outlook and attitude of life at all times. In other words, all of our being is involved in wonder all of the time. This kind of wonder is hard to find these days.

Substitutes for Wonder

Why is there so little true wonder in our world today? One reason is that the world God made is disappointing to most people. In every area of life we seem to see nothing but problems: low wages and high prices, discrimination, political immorality, slums and smog and pollution, hypocrisy—the list is a long one. The good seem to suffer and the bad seem to succeed. It's very easy to develop a "what's-the-use" attitude, become cynical, pull into our own little shell, and let the rest of the world go by.

But the real reason for our present-day loss of wonder goes much deeper. We're living in a mechanical world that's very impersonal. Most people look at the world and think of scientific law instead of a gracious Lawgiver. We are persons, made in the image of God; therefore, we must have a personal world if life is to have any meaning. When life loses its meaning, life loses its wonder; then we become machines! A false view of science and technology has robbed us of a heavenly Father who makes the lilies more glorious than Solomon's wardrobe and who puts out his hand when the sparrow falls.

We live in a mechanical world, and we live in a commercial world. The two questions that seem to control society are "Does it work?" and "Does it pay?" with the emphasis on the latter question. To quote Thoreau again, we have "improved means to unimproved ends." For centuries the philosophers and mystics have been reminding us that we can't enjoy the things that money can buy if we lose the things money can't buy. Making a living has replaced making a life, and searching after new schemes and methods has replaced discovering truth and building character. The very fact of wonder demands values, for we don't wonder at that which is cheap and contemptible. When values vanish, wonder must vanish, too.

Our world is a busy world. We have little time to pause, contemplate, and wonder. Even vacationers pause only long enough to take photos or make videos that they can look at back home when they have more time. They don't have time to get close to people or God's creation, to stand and wonder at what he has made. Quick! Get a picture or two and buy some postcards. We have miles to cover before the day ends!

The child lives in a world of wonder because he stands still long enough to watch and to ponder. Our lives are so full they are perpetually empty. We boast about the quantity of our activity without admitting the lack of quality in our experience. We know how to count activities, but we don't know how to weigh experiences, and we're the losers in the long run.

Perhaps the greatest cause for the lack of wonder is this: we live in an artificial world. Most people are living on substitutes and don't know it. Stupid vulgar comedy has replaced true wit and humor; cheap amusement has replaced wholesome recreation; and propaganda has replaced truth. Millions of bored people depend on manufactured experiences to rescue them from their tedious existence. Each experience must be greater than the previous one, and the result is a nervous system so taxed by substitute stimulants that the person finds it harder and harder to recognize and enjoy an emotional experience that is normal and real. When you exist on artificial stimulants, you gradually lose the ability to recognize and enjoy the real.

The greatest substitute of all is sin, and this is what lies at the root of the whole matter. Unless you and I do something about our sins, we'll never be able to experience and enjoy the wonder that God wants to bring into our lives. The essence of idolatry is worshiping and serving something other than God; living, if you please, on substitutes. But it's a basic law of life that we become like the gods we worship, so if our god is an artificial substitute, we will become artificial too. The very senses that ought to thrill us with wonder become jaded, then paralyzed, then dead. "They have mouths, but they do not speak; eyes they have, but they do not see; they have ears, but they do not hear; noses they have, but they do not smell. . . . Those who make them [the idols] are like them; so is everyone who trusts in them" (Ps. 115:5–6, 8).

The only person who can deal with our basic needs and restore wonder to our lives is Jesus Christ, because his name is Wonderful.

The Wonders of Jesus

Why is Jesus Christ called Wonderful? To name his name is to give the answer, for we would be amazed if he were not called Wonderful! Everything about Jesus Christ makes the believing heart say, "I will now turn aside and see this great sight!"

To start with, he's wonderful in his person. Imagine God coming to earth as man!

> Christ, by highest heaven adored;
> Christ, the Everlasting Lord!
> Late in time behold Him come,
> Offspring of the virgin's womb:
> Veiled in flesh the Godhead see;
> Hail th' Incarnate Deity!
> Pleased as man with man to dwell,
> Jesus, our Emmanuel.
> (Charles Wesley)

When the shepherds shared the news of the birth of Jesus, "all those who heard it marveled at those things which were told them by the shepherds" (Luke 2:18). It was something to wonder at: "God was manifested in the flesh" (1 Tim. 3:16).

Christ was wonderful in the life he lived on earth. Everything that yielded to him participated in wonder. It was just another wedding until Jesus arrived, and he transformed it into a wonderful occasion that is still pondered by devout souls. Ordinary servants put ordinary water into ordinary stone pots and then the extraordinary happened! The wonder of it all—water was transformed into wine! But this is the wonder of his life. Whatever he touched took on new substance and new meaning.

Peter and his fisherman friends would have lived ordinary lives and died ordinary deaths had they never met Jesus; but when Jesus started giving the orders, catching fish was a totally new experience for them. "Launch out into the deep!" "Cast the net on the right side of the ship!" Peter had experienced storms on the Sea of Galilee, but the experience was different when Jesus Christ was in control. "Peace! Be still!" Jesus even empowered Peter to walk on the water!

Whatever Jesus touched, he blessed and beautified and made wonderful. He longed for people to open their eyes to see the world around them: the splendor of the lilies, the freedom of the sparrows, the miracle of the children, the message of the wind. He took everyday bread and wine and gave these necessities a depth of meaning that transformed them into luxuries of God's grace. A little seed suddenly becomes a sermon: "The seed is the Word of God." Water becomes a picture of the Holy Spirit. A lost sheep is a lost soul. He wrote in the dust and confounded the angry religious leaders. Perhaps the greatest wonder of all was his transforming a shameful cross into the meeting place of God's love and man's sin.

Everything about Jesus is wonderful: his birth, his life, and his words. "So all bore witness to Him, and marveled

23

at the gracious words which proceeded out of His mouth" (Luke 4:22). Unlike the scribes, who quoted authorities, Jesus spoke with authority. His teaching was no second-hand tradition; his message was firsthand truth from God. "I speak to the world those things which I heard from Him" (John 8:26). And he practiced what he taught! "Which of you convicts Me of sin?" (John 8:46). In his words we find simplicity—the common people heard him gladly—and yet profundity, a depth of meaning that the greatest minds are still trying to fathom. He was at home with the lowliest peasant or the most learned rabbi.

The greatest wonder of his teaching is that in his words we have life. "The words that I speak to you are spirit, and they are life" (John 6:63). When we read the greatest writings of the ages, our hearts may be stirred and our minds instructed, but when we meditate on the words of Christ, we share in the wonder of his life. His Word feeds the inner person and satisfies. They give much more than enlightenment; they give enablement and help us to live in him.

Consider the wonder of his death. He came to die; he knew he would die; he was willing to die. If any man ever had a right to live, it was Jesus Christ; yet he willingly died, "even the death of the cross" (Phil. 2:8).

> Well might the sun in darkness hide,
> And shut His glories in,
> When Christ the mighty Maker died
> For man the creature's sin.
>
> (Isaac Watts)

Far greater than the three hours of darkness, or the earthquake that rent the tombs, was the loving surrender of the Son of God as he willingly bore the sins of the world on his own body. What wondrous love is this! Add to this the wonder of his resurrection and his ascension, the wonder of the salvation that he purchased for us, and the wonder of the grace he lavishes on us! Oh, my soul! What a wonder he is!

The Wonder of Jesus in Us

Do we need wonder in our lives? Yes, we do; otherwise life becomes bland and blind, dull and dead, and we miss much of what God has prepared for us. The dullness of life isn't caused by circumstances on the outside, but by spiritual conditions on the inside. Jesus lived in the same world as the multitudes that followed him, and yet it was not the same world. Christ's world was a different and more wonderful world. No wonder he lamented, "Seeing they do not see, and hearing they do not hear, nor do they understand" (Matt. 13:13).

Whenever he spoke about the deeper spiritual realities, the people (including his own disciples) thought he was referring to the material things they could see. "Destroy this temple, and in three days I will raise it up" was thought to be referring to the Jewish temple, but "He was speaking of the temple of His body" (John 2:19, 21). "You must be born again," he told Nicodemus, who then asked, "How can a man be born when he is old?" Nicodemus thought of physical birth, but our Lord was speaking of spiritual birth. The woman at the well thought Jesus was speaking of physical water (John 4:11); the crowds in the Capernaum synagogue thought he was speaking about literally eating his flesh and drinking his blood (John 6). Oh, the blindness of those who have no wonder in their hearts!

Wonder is important. That's why his name "Wonderful" leads the list. Unless I know something of his wonder, I'm not likely to come to him for counsel, power, or any other spiritual essential. Wonder leads to worship, and worship to growth, and growth to character and service. Wonder begins with receiving Christ into the heart and life, experiencing the forgiveness of sins, and the invasion of a whole new life. "Christ lives in me" (Gal. 2:20). When we ask him in, Jesus promises, "I will come in to him, and dine with him, and he with Me" (Rev. 3:20).

When you are born again into God's family, you receive a whole new set of spiritual senses, and the inner person is raised from the dead and given divine life. Everything becomes different.

> Heav'n above is softer blue.
> Earth around is sweeter green!
> Something lives in every hue
> Christless eyes have never seen:
> Birds with gladder songs o'erflow.
> Flow'rs with deeper beauty shine.
> Since I know, as now I know,
> I am His, and He is mine.
> (George Wade Robinson)

Wonder comes into your life as you walk with him in obedience and consecration. How much the disciples learned as they listened to him, followed him, and let him guide their lives! There's no substitute for daily fellowship with the Lord in his Word and in prayer, and then walking with him in obedience. This kind of daily experience sharpens the spiritual senses of the inner person. Your eyes begin to see the way he sees; your ears start to hear what he hears; and (most important of all) your heart begins to love what he loves. Your values change as your vision sharpens. Your deepening love for Christ opens new windows and doors for you, and life begins to fulfill the promise of 1 Corinthians 2:9—"Eye has not seen, nor ear heard, nor have entered into the heart of man the things which God

26

has prepared for those who love Him." Wonder is a liberating experience. It breaks the shackles and calls us to a life of faith and love.

This life of wonder with the Wonderful One climaxes in glory: "We know that when He is revealed, we shall be like Him for we shall see Him as he is" (1 John 3:2). Eternal wonder! We will see with perfect vision, love with sinless hearts, and obey with wills that are lost in the wonder of the glory of God! The glory of heaven is its wonder in Christ; the tragedy of hell is the absence of Christ and his wonder. Darkness, dullness, frightening monotony, eternal loneliness, eternal purposelessness, pain and sorrow—this is hell. Pain, yes; judgment, yes; but permeating it all, that awful dullness that sin always brings when that first "pleasure" is gone. To be forsaken by God means that the wonder is taken out of your life for all eternity. Jesus called hell "Gehenna," referring to the garbage dump burning outside Jerusalem. What a tragedy: sinful man ceases to be man and ends up just a piece of junk, a cast-off thing on an eternal garbage heap!

Those who walk with Christ by faith know the meaning of wonder in their daily lives. Ordinary people experience extraordinary things because of the wonder of Christ. These wonders may not be obvious to those outside the family of God, but they're clearly visible to those inside the family. His wonders are seen in so-called little things, such as a flower, or a bird, or a baby's smile. And they're seen in big things as well, such as the courage to say "No" or the strength to keep going when the road is difficult. Little things become big things when they're touched by the wonder of Christ. He can make your life wonderful because his name is Wonderful.

Counselor

"H is name is . . . Counselor." This takes care of the decisions of life. "You will guide me with Your counsel, and afterward receive me to glory" (Ps. 73:24).

Where people turn for help is some indication of their character and faith. One man turns to the local bar where he pours out his troubles into the ears of anybody he thinks will be sympathetic. (But then he has to listen to their troubles!) Others visit "readers" or fortune-tellers, or perhaps pay to have their horoscope cast. Many people talk their problems over with a doctor or a pastor, or perhaps visit a psychologist or other trained counselor.

To the Christian, Jesus Christ is the supreme Counselor. "Lord, to whom shall we go? You have the words of eternal life" (John 6:68). While it's helpful to talk to friends and professional counselors, our first obligation is to talk to the Lord and listen to his Word. The fact that he is called "Counselor" reveals several important truths to us that help us in making the decisions of life.

The Necessity of God's Counsel

You and I need counsel because we don't have within our-selves what it takes to make life work. Many people who know how to make a success out of their careers don't know how to make a success out of their lives, marriages, and homes. "O LORD, I know that the way of man is not in himself; it is not in man who walks to direct his own steps" (Jer. 10:23).

Why people have a difficult time directing their steps isn't difficult to explain. To begin with, our hearts are basi-cally sinful and selfish, and our motives are mixed. Jeremiah says it accurately: "The heart is deceitful above all things, and desperately wicked; who can know it?" (Jer. 17:9). How easy it is to say, "Well, if I know my own heart!" But the plain fact is that we don't know our own hearts! Peter looked into his heart and thought he saw courage and stability, but when Jesus looked into Peter's heart he saw cowardice and failure. "Counsel in the heart of man is like deep water," warns Proverbs 20:5.

Not only is the human heart desperately and deceitfully wicked, but the human mind is severely limited. "For My thoughts are not your thoughts, nor are your ways My ways" (Isa. 55:8). "For who has known the mind of the LORD? Or who has become his counselor?" (Rom. 11:34). As we yield to the Lord and allow his Word to "renew our minds" (Rom. 12:2), we gradually learn more about his character and his ways, and we find it easier to determine his will. But we never come to the place in life where we can ignore prayer and the Scriptures and depend only on our own thinking.

Added to these internal deficiencies—a deceptive heart and a limited mind—are the external pressures of the world and the internal devices of the devil. We're surrounded by an atmosphere created by people who hate God and oppose everything that belongs to a godly life. The world wants us to listen to its counsel, walk in its paths, and adopt its scornful attitude (Ps. 1:1), but God says, "Do not be conformed to this world" (Rom. 12:2).

Satan blinds the minds of unbelievers (2 Cor. 4:1–4) and tries to deceive the minds of believers (2 Cor. 11:1–3). Satan deceived Eve's mind with his lies, and he's been successfully telling the same lies to her sons and daughters ever since. Even Peter was led astray by the devil (Matt. 16:22–23)! God's existence and character are clearly seen in what he's created, but sinners don't even want to retain God in their knowledge (Rom. 1:28). The pressure around us to think the way the world thinks makes it imperative that we seek God's counsel and walk in his way.

Giving counsel to his children is one of God's most gracious works. The very way he does it is evidence of his love and kindness. "If any of you lacks wisdom, let him ask of God, who gives to all liberally and without reproach, and it will be given to him" (James 1:5). Some of God's children would prefer a guidebook, complete with rules, charts, and maps, which they could consult for direction, but God doesn't work that way. If we had a "magic oracle" that always told us what to do, we would never mature and become more like Christ.

My family and I were driving to Canada for a week of ministry. The local auto club provided me with a set of maps that told us everything we needed to know: the roads to take, the construction areas to avoid, the restaurants to visit, and even the "police traps" to watch out for along the way. This approach is fine for an auto trip, but it won't work on the highway of life.

Yes, we have a guidebook—the Bible—but it doesn't tell us exactly who to marry, what city to live in, what job to accept, what school to attend, or a host of other important matters that people must decide about day after day. Along with his Word, God gives us the privilege of prayer and the promised help of the indwelling Holy Spirit. He expects us to use these spiritual resources to make wise decisions. The process isn't simple or easy, but following this process is the way we grow. Praying, meditating, and waiting when we come to Christ, our Counselor, will mature us and strengthen us, and will bring glory to God as we develop our spiritual senses.

The fact that Jesus Christ is the Counselor indicates that he has a definite plan for each life. We aren't left to drift or wander, for he knows where he wants us to be and what he wants us to do. When we seek his counsel, we aren't asking for a luxury; we're seeking a spiritual necessity. We must have the guidance of God if we're to experience the grace of God and manifest the glory of God.

Christ, the Qualified Counselor

Since Jesus Christ is called "Counselor," it means that he is qualified to counsel us. Not every person is so qualified; in fact, it's against the law to advertise your services as a professional counselor unless you possess the necessary credentials. Having an interest in people and being able to give advice are not sufficient credentials in most places. The authorities require a certain amount of education, some practical experience under the guidance of a trained counselor, and proficiency in the field as proved by official examinations.

Is Jesus Christ qualified to be your counselor? Of course he is! For one thing, he is eternal God in whom "dwells all the fullness of the Godhead bodily" (Col. 2:9). Jesus Christ exercised an important ministry in the original creation, for "all things were made through Him" (John 1:3). Jesus was there when the Father said, "Let us make man!" Solomon's "Hymn to Wisdom" in Proverbs 8:22–36 reminds us of Jesus Christ, the eternal Son of God, and the wisdom of God. Paul tells us that in Christ "are hidden all the treasures of wisdom and knowledge" (Col. 2:3). There's nothing he doesn't know!

But something else makes him a qualified counselor: he is also man and understands how we feel. Because he was born into this world as a human, grew up, labored, suffered, and died, he's able to enter into the experiences that perplex and burden you. How many times the professional counselor hears, "Oh, you just don't understand!" But those words can never honestly be spoken to Jesus Christ, because he does understand.

"Therefore, in all things He had to be made like His brethren, that He might be a merciful and faithful High Priest in things pertaining to God. . . . For in that He Himself has suffered, being tempted, He is able to aid those who are tempted" (Heb. 2:17–18).

Consider another fact: Jesus loves us. Counselors are warned not to get involved emotionally with their patients, lest this involvement hinder them from doing their best. But Jesus Christ deals with us in love and always speaks the truth in love (Eph. 4:15). In the upper room, he told Peter the truth about himself, and tried to guide Peter into the place of victory. Unfortunately, Peter rejected the truth, and even argued with it, and the result was shameful failure. Some people hold back the truth because they think this is one way to show love. Others tell the truth but have no love. Jesus Christ is able to blend both truth and love, and this makes him an effective counselor.

As our Counselor, Jesus encourages us and says to us as he said to his disciples, "Let not your heart be troubled" (John 14:1). Why wouldn't their hearts be troubled? He had just told them that Peter would deny him and that one of their number was a traitor! On top of this, he had told them that he was leaving them to go back to the Father. Their hearts were troubled, deeply so, and so he sought to encourage them and prepare them for the demands that lay before them. He told them about the Father's house and about the Holy Spirit, the "Comforter," the "Encourager."

(That's what the word "comfort" really means—"to encourage, to give strength.")

Good counselors don't protect us from the problems of life; instead, they prepare us for life's problems and help us face them honestly and courageously. "Do not pray for easy lives," said Phillips Brooks. "Pray to be stronger men and women. Do not pray for tasks equal to your powers. Pray for powers equal to your tasks."

"God is our refuge and strength, a very present help in trouble" (Ps. 46:1). As our refuge, he hides us; as our strength, he helps us. We don't leave our Counselor's presence merely with good advice. He sends us away with the strength we need to do what he tells us to do.

Jesus Christ, our Counselor, is patient with us. As you read the four Gospels, you can't help but be impressed with our Lord's patience with his disciples as he answers their questions, endures their ignorance and selfishness, and attempts to teach them and prepare them for their life's ministry. Even the best counselors occasionally lose their patience and try to push their clients faster than they're able to go, but not so with the Lord Jesus Christ. "I still have many things to say to you, but you cannot bear them now" (John 16:12). He knows the right time and the right circumstances for revealing a new truth or reminding us of an old truth.

Our heavenly Counselor knows our hearts perfectly. "He knew all men, and had no need that anyone should testify of man, for He knew what was in man" (John 2:24–25). "And all the churches shall know that I am He who searches deep within men's hearts, and minds. . . ." (Rev. 2:23 TLB). "Counsel in the heart of man is like deep water, but a man of understanding will draw it out" (Prov. 20:5). Jesus knows the human heart and mind and is able to help us understand ourselves. What a wonderful Counselor he is!

I would add one final characteristic that shows the greatness of our Counselor: He prays for us. "I do not pray for these alone, but also for those who will believe in Me through their word" (John 17:20). He prays for us constantly, for "He always lives to make intercession for them" (Heb. 7:25). For what does he pray? That we might be made "complete in every good work to do His will" (Heb. 13:21). "For it is God who works in you both to will and to do for His good pleasure" (Phil. 2:13).

You and I need spiritual counsel, and Jesus Christ is perfectly qualified to be our Counselor.

His Counsel in Our Lives

Christ's counsel is available to us now. Providing this counsel is a part of his ministry as our High Priest.

He counsels us through his Word. "Your testimonies also are my delight and my counselors" (Ps. 119:24). Consider the wisdom that God gives us through his Word. "You, through Your commandments, make me wiser than my enemies. . . . I have more understanding than all my teachers. . . . I understand more than the ancients. . . ." (Ps. 119:98–100). We can learn from the Word what other people must learn in the difficult "school of hard knocks." There's no need for God's people to learn the hard way by suffering the bitter consequences of sin. We can learn from the Word, avoid sin, and be the wiser for it.

He also counsels us by his Spirit. "The spirit of the LORD shall rest upon Him, the spirit of wisdom and understanding, the Spirit of counsel and might" (Isa. 11:2). The Spirit of God teaches us from the Word of God. He also teaches us in the everyday experiences of life as he speaks to us from the Word and directs us. "Now when they [Paul and his associates] had gone through Phrygia and the region of Galatia, they were forbidden by the Holy Spirit to preach the word in Asia. After they had come to Mysia, they tried to go into Bithynia, but the Spirit did not permit them" (Acts 16:6–7). How the Holy Spirit directed Paul and his party we don't know, but that he does direct us, we can be sure. Often the Lord uses circumstances to give us counsel and direction. "I will instruct you and teach you in the way you should go; I will guide you with My eye" (Ps. 32:8). "I will counsel you with My eye upon you," reads the New American Standard Bible. What human counselor can keep his or her eye upon the counselees to make sure that they obey? "For the eyes of the LORD are on the righteous, and His ears are open to their prayers" (1 Peter 3:12). The child of God learns that his Father is in control of circumstances, and that the things that happen often point the way to the will of God.

Our Counselor will often use other people to help direct us. "Ointment and perfume delight the heart, and the sweetness of a man's friend does so by hearty counsel" (Prov. 27:9). This is one of the blessings of Christian fellowship in the local gathering of believers: we're able to encourage and admonish one another in the will of God. We must be careful, of course, to listen only to *wise* counselors. King Rehoboam listened to his young friends, and the results for him and the kingdom were tragic (1 Kings 12).

So, our Counselor directs us by his Word, his Spirit, the circumstances of life, and through the believers with whom we fellowship. But what must we do so that God might share his counsel with us? We must be willing to do what he says. "If any of you really determines to do God's will, then you will certainly know whether my teaching is from God or is merely my own" (John 7:17 TLB). God doesn't give his counsel to the curious or the careless; he reveals his will to the concerned and the consecrated. Some believers take the attitude, "I'll ask God what he wants me to do, and if I like it, I'll do it." The result is predictable: God doesn't speak to them. Unless we have a serious desire both to know and to do the counsel of God, he will not reveal his will to us.

35

We Must Seek God's Counsel

"My son, if you receive my words, and treasure my commands within you; so that you incline your ear to wisdom, and apply your heart to understanding; yes, if you cry out for discernment, and lift up your voice for understanding, if you seek her as silver, and search for her as for hidden treasures; then you will understand the fear of the LORD, and find the knowledge of God" (Prov. 2:1–5).

Sad to say, many times people have come to me for spiritual counsel without a sincere desire to seek the mind and will of God. They were impatient; they wanted me to hand them a prepackaged plan. They were unwilling to discipline themselves in Bible study and prayer to diligently seek the wisdom God had for them. They expected to find nuggets of truth lying on the surface of life, and were unwilling to dig for the hidden treasures.

Desire God's counsel, seek it, and wait for it. This unwillingness to wait on the Lord was what led Israel into disobedience time after time. "They soon forgot His works; they did not wait for His counsel" (Ps. 106:13). A teacher can instruct a pupil in algebra and answer his questions immediately, but in the school of life, our Counselor must wait until we are ready for the answer. "I still have many things to say to you, but you cannot bear them now" (John 16:12). God's delays are preparation for God's blessings. If you don't know what God wants you to do, wait patiently and keep doing what he's told you to do. Your gracious Counselor will never lead you astray, but you can lead yourself astray if you become impatient and impulsive. "He who believes will not act hastily" (Isa. 28:16).

When the Lord shows you his counsel, gratefully accept it. Don't argue with it; don't ask him to revise it; don't look for a second opinion. Simply accept whatever God tells you to do. God's will isn't given to us for our critical approval;

it's given for our obedient acceptance. There's no "money-back guarantee" if we aren't completely satisfied.

We must accept God's will, and then obey it. The blessing doesn't come in the discovery of God's will, but in the doing of God's will. "But be doers of the word, and not hearers only, deceiving yourselves" (James 1:22). The blessing comes in the doing, not in the hearing (James 1:25). God's standard is "doing the will of God from the heart" (Eph. 6:6).

Your Counselor knows the decisions you must make and how important those decisions are to you and to him. God is lovingly wrapped up in your life. He has a tremendous investment in you and your future. He has more to lose if you fail than you do, for his eternal glory is at stake. He wants to be your Counselor and show you his will. He doesn't want to counsel you only in the emergencies of life; he wants to counsel you every day in even the mundane things of life. "Therefore, whether you eat or drink, or whatever you do, do all to the glory of God" (1 Cor. 10:31). As you seek his counsel, you get to know him better. In knowing him better, you better understand his will.

God's counsel must never be separated from God's character, for his person and his plan always go together. "He cannot deny Himself" (2 Tim. 2:13). The more two persons love each other, the more they involve each other in the plans and activities of life. Your Counselor wants to be a part of every area of your life, for as you walk together, you better understand his character and his will.

God doesn't need our counsel; we need his. "For who has known the mind of the LORD? Or who has been His counselor?" (Rom. 11:34). Too often we come to him and tell him what he ought to do, when we should wait before him quietly and let him counsel us. "Speak, LORD, for Your servant hears" (1 Sam. 3:9). "This is the way, walk in it" (Isa. 30:21).

There's no need to fear the decisions of life when you know Jesus Christ, for his name is Counselor.

THE MIGHTY GOD

is name is "Mighty God," and this takes care of the demands of life. "For He who is mighty has done great things for me, and holy is His name" (Luke 1:49).

The history of mankind has been the story of the discovery and application of power. First it was manpower, then horsepower, then steam power and electric power, and now atomic power. Each step on the "power path" has enriched mankind materially and financially, but it's doubtful that we are any richer spiritually. We're able to harness the powers of the universe, but we can't control ourselves or keep selfish people from destroying the world and its people. We're still weaklings when it comes to the things that matter most. I'm sure some future historian will call the last half of the twentieth century "The Age of Power and Weakness."

The basic power needed today is spiritual power, and the source of that power is Jesus Christ. He is the "Mighty God."

He Is God

The fact that Jesus Christ is called "Mighty God" indicates that he is God. Leo Tolstoy wrote: "I believe Christ was a man like ourselves; to look upon him as God would seem to me the greatest of sacrileges." And yet Jesus claimed to be God. He dared to say, "That all should honor the Son just as they honor the Father. He who does not honor the Son does not honor the Father who sent Him" (John 5:23). At the close of his sermon on the Good Shepherd, Jesus said boldly, "I and My Father are one" (John 10:30). The people present understood this statement to be a clear claim to deity, and they responded by picking up stones to stone him!

Near the close of his public ministry, just before his death on the cross, Jesus cried out, "He who believes in Me, believes not in Me but in Him who sent Me. And he who sees Me sees Him who sent Me" (John 12:44–45). He told Philip, "He who has seen Me has seen the Father" (John 14:9). In plain, simple language Jesus Christ claimed to be God.

Those who knew him affirmed that he was God. The apostle John identified Jesus as "the Word" and wrote: "In the beginning was the Word, and the Word was with God, and the Word was God" (John 1:1). Thomas fell before Jesus in worship and exclaimed, "My Lord and my God!" (John 20:28), and Jesus didn't correct him. If any man opposed the idea that Jesus of Nazareth was God in the flesh, it was Saul of Tarsus. When he met Jesus, however, the zealous rabbi changed his mind and was for the rest of his life a witness to the deity of Jesus Christ. Paul wrote concerning his nation, Israel, "Of whom are the fathers, and from whom according to the flesh, Christ came, who is over all, the eternally blessed God. Amen" (Rom. 9:5). Titus 2:13 says, "Looking for that blessed hope, and glorious appearing of our great God and Savior Jesus Christ."

A member of a cult that denies the deity of Christ challenged me one day with, "You can't find one verse in the

Bible that calls Jesus 'God'!" I turned to Hebrews 1:8: "But to the Son He says, 'Your throne, O God, is forever and ever.'" The man's only reply was to refer me to another translation that obviously twisted the original language in order to support false doctrine.

Referring to Jesus Christ, the apostle John writes: "This is the true God and eternal life" (1 John 5:20). You don't have to be a Greek scholar to understand that statement. Jesus claimed to be God and accepted that claim from the lips of others. He accepted worship as God. He also claimed to do things that only God can do, such as forgive sins (Luke 7:49).

The names that he bears affirm his deity. The very name "Jesus" means "Jehovah is salvation"; while many people in his time bore that name (in tribute to the great leader Joshua), Jesus actually lived up to it. He said to Zacchaeus, "Today salvation has come to this house. . . ." (Luke 19:9). Jesus forgave the sins of the paralytic, and the religious leaders exclaimed, "Why does this Man speak blasphemies like this? Who can forgive sins but God alone?" (Mark 2:7).

One of his names is "Immanuel" which means "God with us" (Matt. 1:23). The angel identified him to Mary: "that Holy One who is to be born will be called the Son of God" (Luke 1:35). Mary was the one witness who could have saved Jesus from the cross. Yet she stood at the cross and made no protest. If Jesus was not God, why was Mary silent?

Since Jesus is God, he deserves our faith, love, obedience, service, and worship. "Because He is your Lord, worship Him" (Ps. 45:11). To reject Christ is to reject God, and to reject God is to reject life. "He who believes in the Son has everlasting life: and he who does not believe the Son shall not see life, but the wrath of God abides on him" (John 3:36). "After six years given to the impartial investigation of Christianity," wrote General Lew Wallace, author of *Ben Hur,* "as to its truth or falsity, I have come to the deliberate conclusion that Jesus Christ was the Messiah of the Jews, the Savior of the world, and my personal Savior."

Jesus cannot be avoided; we must face the facts about him and decide. Isaiah says that Jesus is God. What do you say?

Christ's Power Revealed

Not only is Jesus called God, but he is called the "Mighty God." What a paradox that a babe in a manger should be called mighty! Yet even as a babe, Jesus Christ was the center of power. His birth affected the heavens and caused a dazzling star to appear. The star aroused the interest of the Magi, and they left their homes and made a long and perilous journey to Jerusalem. Their announcement about the newborn King unnerved Herod and his court. Jesus' birth brought angels from heaven and simple shepherds from their flocks on the hillside. Midnight became midday as the glory of the Lord appeared to men.

We also see the mighty power of Jesus Christ in the creation of the universe. "All things were made through Him, and without Him nothing was made that was made" (John 1:3). Obviously, then, he himself was not created since he made *everything* that was made. No statement in Scripture puts it more majestically than Hebrews 1:1–3: "God, who at various times and in different ways spoke in times past to the fathers by the prophets, has in these last days spoken to us by His Son, whom He has appointed heir of all things, through whom also He made the worlds; who being the brightness of His glory and the express image of His person, and upholding all things by the word of His power, when He had by Himself purged our sins, sat down at the right hand of the Majesty on high."

The apostle Paul agrees with this statement. "He is the image of the invisible God, the firstborn over all creation. For by Him all things were created that are in heaven and that are on earth, visible and invisible. . . . All things were created through Him and for Him" (Col. 1:15–16). What mystery: the Creator becomes a creature! He who fills all things becomes an infant in a cattle stall! The mighty God!

Not only does Jesus reveal his power in creation, but also in history. The Bethlehem promise tells us this: "But you, Bethlehem Ephrathah, though you are little among the thousands of Judah, yet out of you shall come forth to Me the One to be ruler in Israel, whose goings forth have been from old, from everlasting" (Micah 5:2).

Old Testament history is the story of his goings forth. As Dr. A. T. Pierson used to put it, "History is His story." No matter where you turn in the Old Testament record, you meet Jesus Christ. "Your father Abraham rejoiced to see My day," said Jesus to the Jewish leaders, "and he saw it and was glad" (John 8:56). Moses accomplished what he did because he esteemed "the reproach of Christ greater riches than the treasures in Egypt" (Heb. 11:26). Before conquering the city of Jericho, Joshua met Jesus the commander one night and bowed before him in worship (Josh. 5:13–15). The three Hebrew children walked with him in the fiery furnace (Dan. 3:24–25). No wonder the Lord Jesus was able to teach those discouraged Emmaus disciples from the Old Testament, for it records his goings forth! "And beginning at Moses and all the Prophets, He expounded to them in all the Scriptures the things concerning Himself" (Luke 24:27).

When he ministered here on earth, Jesus revealed himself as the "Mighty God" by the miracles that he performed. The very accomplishment of these works was evidence of his deity and left the beholders without excuse. "Then He began to rebuke the cities in which most of His mighty works had been done, because they did not repent" (Matt. 11:20). His fellow countrymen marveled "that such mighty works" were performed by his hands (Mark 6:2). And yet they failed to trust him! "Now He could do no mighty work there, except that He laid His hands on a few sick people and healed them" (Mark 6:5).

His enemies argued that Christ's power originated from Satan; but that was only an evasion of facts. He quickly demolished their argument. "If Satan casts out Satan, he is divided against himself. How then will his kingdom stand?" (Matt. 12:26).

Of course, the greatest act of power that he performed on this planet involved his death and resurrection. Paul prayed for the Ephesians (and for us) that they might know "what is the exceeding greatness of His power toward us who believe, according to the working of His mighty power which He worked in Christ when He raised Him from the dead and seated Him at His right hand in the heavenly places" (Eph. 1:19–20). God raised Jesus from the dead "having loosed the pains of death, because it was not possible that He should be held by it" (Acts 2:24).

Not only did the Father raise Jesus from the dead, but Jesus raised himself from the dead! Speaking about his life, Jesus said, "I have power to lay it down, and I have power to take it again" (John 10:18). "For as the Father has life in Himself, so He has granted the Son to have life in Himself" (John 5:26).

The miracle of his resurrection is central to his work of redemption. The gospel message says "that Christ died for our sins according to the Scriptures, and that He was buried, and that He rose again the third day according to the Scriptures" (1 Cor. 15:3–4). His resurrection guarantees our redemption. "In Him we have redemption through His blood, the forgiveness of sins, according to the riches of His grace" (Eph. 1:7).

It's unfortunate that some of the pictures artists draw of Jesus (and no picture of him is authentic) depict him as something less than a man. Certainly he was meek, but meekness isn't weakness. Meekness is power under control. He was lowly in heart, but he was able to make a whip of cords and drive the hypocritical money-changers out of the temple. His arrest and crucifixion appear to be experiences of weakness, and in one sense they are, but in a deeper sense, they reveal his mighty power. "For though He was crucified in weakness, yet He lives by the power of God" (2 Cor. 13:4). No wonder Paul shouts, "I can do all things through Christ who strengthens me" (Phil. 4:13).

Jesus Christ is God, and he is "Mighty God." But what does this mean to us today who believe in him?

God's Power in Us

His mighty power is available to us today. Here is the way Paul prays for people like us: "For this reason we also, since the day we heard it, do not cease to pray for you, and to ask that you may be filled with the knowledge of His will in all wisdom and spiritual understanding; that you may have a walk worthy of the Lord, fully pleasing Him, being fruitful in every good work and increasing in the knowledge of God; strengthened with all might, according to His glorious power, for all patience and longsuffering with joy" (Col. 1:9–11).

Note the universals in that prayer: all wisdom, fully pleasing, every good work, all might. If God fills us with "all might," then that makes us almighty! We are strengthened with all might! We have no problem believing that Jesus Christ is almighty, but to assign this attribute to his people—mere creatures of clay—is a great leap of faith. But it's true: the almighty power of God is available to us through Jesus Christ. Salvation is not something that God begins and we finish.

Salvation is the work of God from start to finish. "Being confident of this very thing, that He who has begun a good work in you will complete it until the day of Jesus Christ" (Phil. 1:6). On the cross, Jesus cried, "It is finished!" He provides a complete salvation. He didn't "make the down payment" and expect us to keep up the installments! No, "It is finished!"

This means that God's believing people can claim from Christ all that they need. "And my God shall supply all your need according to His riches in glory by Christ Jesus" (Phil. 4:19). But note that Paul's prayer in Colossians 1 deals with the inner person, the character of the believer, and not the material or physical needs of life: "Strengthened with all might . . . for all patience and longsuffering with joy." The almighty power of God is available to us through Jesus Christ so that we might develop Christian character and practice Christian conduct to the glory of God. Patience, longsuffering, and joy don't come to our lives automatically; it takes spiritual power to produce this kind of godly character.

Paul himself is a good example of what the power of God can do in our lives. Paul was given a thorn in the flesh (2 Cor. 12:7–10). We don't know what it was, but we know that it was severe enough and painful enough for him to pray three times that God might take it away. Paul's prayer seems logical. After all, he was an important man with a great work to do. Physical pain and weakness would only hinder his ministry.

As you read Paul's account of this experience, you detect several levels of spiritual understanding. First, Paul tried to *escape* the thorn, but God refused to remove it. Then Paul determined to *endure* the thorn, but that was not the level that glorified God the most. Even an unsaved person can courageously endure pain. God's grace moved Paul to a higher level: he *accepted* his pain, then learned to triumph in it! "Therefore most gladly I rather boast in my infirmities, that the power of Christ may rest upon me" (v. 9). He learned to be enriched and empowered by the weakness that his handicap brought to his life. The secret? "My grace is sufficient for you, for My strength is made perfect in weakness" (v. 9).

Only the grace of God can bring the power of God to our lives. Paul confessed it openly: "But by the grace of God I am what I am" (1 Cor. 15:10). God's grace is channeled to our lives through God's Son, Jesus Christ. "And of His fullness we have all received, and grace for grace" (John 1:16). Through grace God does in and through us what we could never do for ourselves. Grace isn't simply a supplement to our strength, for we have no strength of our own. Grace turns our weakness into power for the glory of God. "For when I am weak, then I am strong" (2 Cor. 12:10). The reason many people don't experience God's power is because they're too strong in themselves and won't confess their weakness. God has to wait until they're weak; then he can share his power with them.

The Bible contains many examples of this principle of weakness turned into strength. When Abraham was seventy-five years old, God promised to give him a son through whom a great nation would be built and the whole world blessed (Gen. 12:1–3). Ten years passed, and the son hadn't yet been given. Abraham's wife Sarah suggested that her husband take her handmaid, Hagar, and have a son by her; Abraham cooperated with the plan. Hagar did bear a son, but the whole enterprise was contrary to God's will and led to serious family problems. God waited another thirteen years, until Abraham was ninety-nine years old, before he began to fulfill his promise. And when Abraham was one hundred years old, and his wife ninety, the son Isaac was born.

Romans 4:19–21 explains the great miracle: "And not being weak in faith, he [Abraham] did not consider his own body, already dead (since he was about a hundred years old), and the deadness of Sarah's womb. He did not waver at the promise of God through unbelief, but was strengthened in faith, giving glory to God, and being fully convinced that what He had promised He was also able to perform."

It was Abraham's faith that released the power of God in his life. He didn't look at circumstances or depend on personal feelings. He simply claimed the almighty power of God and God released his power and, as it were, raised Abraham and Sarah from the dead! God's promises and

God's performances go together. "There has not failed one word of all His good promise" (1 Kings 8:56).

What God did for Abraham and Sarah he also did for Moses, Gideon, David, Daniel, Peter, Paul, and myriads of believing people whose names are found in the pages of the Bible and church history. God worked in them and through them, and they did exploits and brought glory to Christ. God is still looking for believing people who can become channels of his almighty power in a world that is characterized by weakness. "For the eyes of the LORD run to and fro throughout the whole earth, to show Himself strong on behalf of those whose heart is loyal to Him" (2 Chron. 16:9). A loyal heart doesn't mean a sinless heart, for nobody alive has a sinless heart. It means a heart completely trusting in the Lord, a heart that is not divided in its loyalty. The Lord doesn't entrust his power to those who will not trust him completely.

Whatever may be your burden or battle today, God has the power to meet it, handle it, solve it, and use it for your good and his glory. Jesus Christ is the "Mighty God" and his power is available to you. "Now to Him who is able to do exceedingly abundantly above all that we ask or think, according to the power that works in us. . . ." (Eph. 3:20). Admit your own weakness, yield to him by faith, and receive his promised power.

THE EVERLASTING FATHER

Our Lord's name is "Everlasting Father" and this takes care of the dimensions of life. "I have come that they may have life, and that they may have it more abundantly" (John 10:10).

That Jesus Christ, the Son of God, should be called "Everlasting Father" appears to be a theological contradiction; if Jesus is the Son, he can't be the Father. Each member of the Godhead—the Father and the Son and the Holy Spirit—is separate from the other members and yet equally God. The Father is not the Son and the Son is not the Father.

The answer, of course, is in the unique use of the word "father" by the Semitic peoples. An Old Testament Jew reading Isaiah's prophecy would recognize the word "father" to mean "originator of" or "author of." Jesus called Satan the "father of lies" (John 8:44), and Jabal was called the "father of those who dwell in tents and have livestock" (Gen. 4:20). In calling Jesus Christ the "Everlasting Father," the prophet was saying, "He is the originator of that which is everlasting. He is the author of the eternal."

Eternity

Eternity is a concept so vast in its scope that the human mind can't even begin to grasp it. That which is eternal has neither beginning nor ending, and God is eternal. Man has a beginning, but no ending. Man will live forever, either with God or apart from God, either in eternal glory or eternal darkness. The Puritan preacher Thomas Watson said, "Eternity to the godly is a day that has no sunset; eternity to the wicked is a night that has no sunrise."

When you trust Jesus Christ to save you from your sins, you become a part of eternity; you receive the gift of eternal life. Jesus has "fathered" eternity in the lives of all who have trusted him, and this involves much more than simply having our sins forgiven and knowing that we have a home in heaven. Those who belong to Christ have become a part of the very life of God and have entered forever into the realm of the eternal.

Because Jesus Christ is "Wonderful," he takes care of the dullness of life. As the "Counselor," he handles the decisions of life. The "Mighty God" enables you to meet the demands of life, and the "Everlasting Father" provides new dimensions to your life. You are part of the eternal.

Made for Eternity

God made us for eternity. "He has made everything appropriate in its time. He has also set eternity in their heart, without which men will not find out the work which God has done from the beginning even to the end" (Eccl. 3:11 NASB, see margin). This verse seems to suggest that God made man's heart so that man is dissatisfied with life on the surface and has a deep craving for that which is changeless and eternal.

In our higher and better moments, we know that there's something more than this brief physical life, that we are made for something greater than what time can offer, and we search for this missing dimension. In one sense, all of man's quests in science, philosophy, exploration, and even religion are evidences of this deep thirst for the eternal. How many people have died yearning for another lifetime in which to accomplish what they wanted to do! Like the architect of British colonialism in South Africa, Cecil Rhodes, they die saying, "So much left undone!"

Yes, we were made for eternity, and we can't be truly happy and satisfied until we're sharing in eternity. Life is swift and brief, and a man of depth always wants to accomplish more. How you solve this tension between time and eternity determines your philosophy of life and your religious faith. Some people do away with eternity and the God of eternity and live only for time. But then they lose depth and inspiration because they know that a creature like man is made for something grander than three score years and ten. If this philosophy is taken to its logical limits, it leads to, "Eat, drink, and be merry, for tomorrow we die!" If there is no God and no eternity, then why bother to make the most of today? Get it over with as quickly as possible!

Is there any solution to this tension between time and eternity? Yes, there is: Jesus Christ, the eternal Son of God.

When Eternity Invaded Time

God created us for eternity, and Jesus Christ came to earth to reveal and to share the eternal. "That which was from the beginning, which we have heard, which we have seen with our eyes, which we have looked upon, and our hands have handled, concerning the Word of life—the life was manifested, and we have seen, and bear witness, and declare to you that eternal life which was with the Father and was manifested to us" (1 John 1:1–2).

Certainly the eternal God was revealed in creation and in the giving of the Law, but each of those revelations had its limitations. Creation reveals the existence of God and that he has power and wisdom, but creation says little or nothing about the love of God or the grace of God. The Law reveals that God is holy and just, and that he desires his people to be holy, but the Law can't change the sinner's heart or control his motives and actions. God has revealed himself in the events of history and shown his people that he cares, but even here the revelation in history lacks the personal touch that man so needs.

In sending his Son to earth, God caused eternity to invade time. This was not a temporary visit; when Jesus came, he wedded dust and deity, time and eternity, into one. The eternal Word was made human flesh, and that union will last forever. As the perfect man here on earth, Jesus Christ showed us what it is like to live by and for the eternal. He lived as no other man lived, and even the publicans and sinners saw that he was different. As you read the Gospel records, you see the eternal Son moving in the world of time, proving that the eternal is real and satisfying.

Jesus was not simply born; he "came into the world." He invaded time from eternity. His words are "words of eternal life" (John 6:68). His deeds had in them the quality of the eternal. He spoke as no man ever spoke, and he lived as no man ever lived. His values were vastly different from those of contemporary religious leaders, and because of this he challenged the established religious system. Jesus looked at people through the eyes of the eternal and never permitted himself to be shackled by the passing opinions of time. The publicans and sinners weren't outcasts to him; they were lost sheep needing the care of a shepherd, sick people needing a physician. Jesus wasn't impressed with the stones of the temple because he was building a temple that would last forever. When he looked at the lily or saw a sparrow fall, Jesus thought of the eternal Father in heaven.

Almost everything Jesus talked about or touched took on a new dimension because he is the "Father of Eternity." Ordinary bread and wine were touched by eternity when Jesus blessed, broke, and shared, saying, "This is my body, broken for you; this cup is the new covenant in my blood." When he rebuked his overprotective disciples and said, "Permit the little children to come to me," he lifted childhood to its highest level. "Unless you are converted and become as little children, you will by no means enter the kingdom of heaven" (Matt. 18:3).

God made us for eternity; there's more to life than what meets the eye. In Jesus Christ, we see eternity revealed because he is our eternal life. But how do you and I experience the eternal? After all, we're sinners, and sinners receive eternal death, not eternal life (Rev. 20:11–15). Everything that partakes of sin leads to death, so, until you and I can remove this terrible thing called sin, we can never move into the marvelous dimension of the eternal.

When Time and Eternity Met

Jesus came to earth to reveal the eternal, and he died that we might share the eternal. "For God so loved the world, that He gave His only begotten Son, that whoever believes in Him should not perish but have everlasting life" (John 3:16).

Sin is the great obstacle to our experiencing eternal life. Sin isn't eternal; only God is eternal. Sin is outside God and therefore produces death, for God is eternal life. Our nature partakes of sin and therefore is a stranger to the eternal. We were created in the image of God, and there is a hunger for eternity in our hearts. Until we do something about our sins, however, we will never share his eternal life.

God solved the sin problem for us when he sent his Son to die on the cross. Time and eternity met at Calvary. Jesus Christ is the Lamb of God "foreordained before the foundation of the world" (1 Peter 1:20) and "slain from the foundation of the world" (Rev. 13:8). God's great plan of salvation was no hasty afterthought; his people were chosen in Christ "before the foundation of the world" (Eph. 1:4), "according to the eternal purpose which He accomplished in Christ Jesus our Lord" (Eph. 3:11).

When Jesus Christ was born at Bethlehem, time and eternity met in a person, a gift that was given. When he died at Calvary, time and eternity met in a price that was paid, and that price met the demands of God's holy law and opened the way for sinners to be forgiven and share in eternity.

Mere religion can never take away sins or give the sinner a share in eternity. Religion belongs to time; we need a Savior who breaks into time from eternity and who is able to take away our sins. We have such a Savior in Jesus Christ. He is "the author of eternal salvation to all who obey Him" (Heb. 5:9). By the shedding of his blood, he "obtained eternal redemption" for us (Heb. 9:12), and he has promised us an "eternal inheritance" (Heb. 9:15). When we trust him, he gives us the gift of eternal life. "And I give them eternal life, and they shall never perish; neither shall anyone snatch them out of My hand" (John 10:28).

In order to become the "Father of Eternity" to us, he had to suffer on the cross. Our birth into eternal life required his death. The gift of eternal life was not purchased cheaply.

A Life of Eternity

But Jesus Christ is the "Father of Eternity" in another way. He lives now to give eternal purpose and quality to our everyday lives. Sin is the great waster; Satan is the great destroyer. Most of the people in the world are merely existing, not living. What they live on and live for doesn't satisfy fully and can never last eternally. The vast majority of people live on substitutes, and the substitutes are robbing them of the true experiences of life that God wants them to enjoy. Instead of investing time into eternity and enjoying satisfying dividends here and now, most people are only "spending" time or wasting time, and thereby robbing themselves of the eternal. The person who trusts Jesus Christ is unwilling to give so great a price for so small a return.

For the Christian, Jesus Christ is the controller of time. "My times are in Your hand" (Ps. 31:15). Jesus himself lived that way when he ministered here on earth. You can't read the Gospel of John without realizing that he lived according to a divine timetable. "My hour has not yet come," he said to Mary at the beginning of his ministry (John 2:4). To his brothers he said, "My time has not yet come, but your time is always ready" (John 7:6). The unbeliever has no compelling divine schedule to follow. When his enemies tried to arrest Jesus, they found it was impossible "because His hour had not yet come" (John 7:30). The religious leaders wanted to arrest him while he was preaching in the temple, but they failed because "His hour had not yet come" (John 8:20). When Jesus announced that he was returning to Judea because Mary and Martha needed him, his disciples were amazed and afraid. "Rabbi," they protested, "lately the Jews sought to stone You!" His reply revealed the quiet confidence of his heart in the plan and purpose of the Father: "Are there not twelve hours in the day?" (John 11:8–9). In other words, "I'm not walking by sight, but by faith. My Father has a plan and I will follow it."

The climax came in the Garden of Gethsemane when he made that final surrender as he faced the cross: "Father, the hour has come!" (John 17:1).

"My times are in your hand!" Does God still plan for his own and guide them through life? Yes, he does! Is it reasonable that the God who created time at the beginning should abandon his magnificent creation until the final day of judgment? According to Hebrews 1:2, Jesus Christ "framed the ages" (literal translation). This means that even the ages of history are under his control. David looked back and wrote, "I have been young, and now am old; yet I have not seen the righteous forsaken, nor his descendants begging bread" (Ps. 37:25).

At the end of their pilgrimage, the saints of God can look back and see the hand of God at work all the days of their lives. This doesn't mean that everything done was in the will of God, or that there were no detours; but it does mean that God ruled and overruled in their lives to accomplish his eternal purposes.

The fact that Jesus Christ controls time reveals the importance of prayer and the Word of God in our lives. As we fellowship with God, he speaks to us and reveals what he wants us to do. When we pray, we lay hold of eternity. The heart and mind, yielded to the Spirit, become the meeting place of time and eternity. We can honestly say, "My times are in your hands."

Not only does Jesus Christ control time, but he conquers time. For the unbeliever, time is an enemy; for the dedicated Christian, time is a friend. Jesus Christ entered into time that he might save us and accomplish God's eternal purposes in our lives (Eph. 2:8–10). Time became our ally, not our enemy.

How does time fight against people? One way is by delay. Men cannot control time. The seconds, minutes, and hours move along at their appointed pace; man can do nothing to hinder or change it. The child wants to hasten time; the elderly may want to slow it down. The suffering cry out, "How long, O Lord, how long?" Some people, like Peter Pan, want to stop time and remain in the so-called innocent joys of childhood. Others want to speed time along so they can enjoy the pleasures of adulthood. Time is difficult to define, impossible to control.

But the Christian never worries about delay, because his times are in the hands of God. As he contemplated the sorrow of his dear friends at Bethany, Jesus said, "Are there not twelve hours in the day?" In fact, Jesus deliberately delayed his trip to Bethany so that Lazarus had been in the grave four days by the time he arrived. Jesus went through life unafraid because his times were in the hands of the Father. You and I can go through life with this same confidence, because he has conquered time.

We need not fear delay, and we need not fear decay, which is time's second weapon. The hymn writer wrote, "Change and decay in all around I see."[1] Change and decay are enemies that most people fear. Psalm 90 is a vivid description of the ravages of time as contrasted with the calm changelessness of our eternal God. In his majestic paraphrase of that psalm, Isaac Watts writes:

> Time, like an ever-rolling stream,
> Bears all its sons away,
> They fly, forgotten, as a dream
> Dies at the op'ning day.

When we're young, change is a treat; as we grow older, change becomes a threat. But when Jesus Christ is in control of your life, you need never fear change or decay. Paul knew this secret when he wrote: "For our light affliction, which is but for a moment, is working for us a far more exceeding and eternal weight of glory, while we do not look at the things which are seen, but at the things which are not seen. For the things which are seen are temporary, but the things which are not seen are eternal" (2 Cor. 4:17–18). When you're part of the eternal, the decay of the material only hastens the perfecting of the spiritual, if you walk by faith in Christ.

Time's ultimate weapon is death, and Jesus Christ has conquered that enemy as well. This is why Paul can shout triumphantly, "O Death, where is your sting? O Hades, where is your victory?" (1 Cor. 15:55). Man has invented ways to overcome delay and decay, but he has yet to conquer death. Only Jesus Christ can do that. "I am the resurrection and the life!" he said, and then he proved it by raising Lazarus from the grave (John 11:25–26, 43–44).

In that dramatic scene at Bethany, we see the Lord defeating all three of time's weapons. He defeated delay by waiting two days before setting out for Bethany. By the time he arrived, Lazarus had begun to decay, so much so that his sister protested, "Lord, by this time there is a stench, for he has been dead four days" (John 11:39). But Jesus overcame decay and death, for he raised his friend from the dead and restored him to his loved ones again. Jesus Christ has completely conquered time!

Jesus is able to conquer time because he is eternal: "I am the Alpha and the Omega, the Beginning and the End" (Rev. 21:6). He is not limited by time or space because he dwells in eternity. He is above time and therefore is able to conquer and control time. Because he entered into time, he is able to bring eternity into our little lives and move us into a vast new dimension of experience. "He who does the will of God abides forever" (1 John 2:17).

Time flows from the future (tomorrow) into the present (today) and then into the past (yesterday). Man comes out of the past; only God lives in the future. The present, then, is the meeting of the future and the past, and that meeting can be fraught with either triumph or tragedy. When Jesus Christ is in control of your life, each moment has eternal significance because he gives us a quality of life that comes out of eternity.

"Eternal life" means much more than living forever, for even the lost are going to exist forever. "Eternal life" means "the life of eternity." It's the experience we have in Christ here and now!

Jesus Christ made us for eternity. To reject him is to miss the very purpose for which we were created. He came to earth to reveal eternity, and he died to give us eternal life. He lives to make eternity a real and exciting experience for us day by day, as he controls and conquers time.

But there's another ministry that he performs as the "Father of Eternity." One day he will return to take us to a glorious eternal home where there will be no time, no delay, no decay, and no death.

When Time Is No More

Salvation from sin through faith in Christ is not the end; it's the beginning. The best is yet to come! "For the Lord Himself will descend from heaven with a shout, with the voice of an archangel, and with the trumpet of God. And the dead in Christ will rise first. Then we who are alive and remain shall be caught up together with them in the clouds to meet the Lord in the air. And thus shall we always be with the Lord" (1 Thess. 4:16–17). "In a moment, in the twinkling of an eye, at the last trumpet. For the trumpet will sound, and the dead will be raised incorruptible, and we shall be changed" (1 Cor. 15:52).

For us, this last change will be the final change. Time will be no more. We shall share in eternity in our completeness, with a glorious new body that will know nothing of decay or death. We will live with Christ in the eternal now. The lost, sad to say, will be separated from God forever, experiencing the second death, eternal death. Such is the tragedy of life without Christ.

58

As the eternal Holy Spirit works in our lives, we participate in the eternal plan and work of God. As we obey his Word, our lives take on the quality of the eternal. We live in time, but we live for eternity. "He who does the will of God abides forever" (1 John 2:17). Life is neither "spent" nor wasted; life is invested in the eternal. No matter what we experience in life, as we walk by faith it becomes part of an eternal investment that will glorify God forever. The eternal is so glorious that the temporal with its burdens and problems doesn't discourage us or defeat us. The outward person is perishing, but the inward person is being renewed day by day.

Jesus Christ is the "Father of Eternity." As your Savior and Lord, let him give birth to the eternal in your life. "For what will it profit a man if he gains the whole world, and loses his own soul?" (Mark 8:36).

PRINCE OF PEACE

His name is "Prince of Peace," and believing this can take care of the disturbances of life. Jesus still says to his followers, "Peace I leave with you, My peace I give to you" (John 14:27).

Like most important words, "peace" has become all things to all men. A loving mother looks upon the face of her sleeping infant and thinks of peace. A poet looks across the headstones in an old graveyard and thinks of peace. Yet who would exchange the potential of a growing infant for the frozen, silent solemnity of a cemetery?

The Old Testament Jew knew the meaning of the word "peace" even if he didn't always actually experience it. To him the word "peace" (shalom) meant far more than silence or the absence of war. Peace was something living and vibrant that made for the well-being of mankind. Peace meant (as Dr. George Morrison expresses it) "the possession of adequate resources." It has nothing to do with the situation on the outside; it has everything to do with the condition on the inside.

I've watched people sitting in the quiet beauty of nature, growing restless with inactivity, smoking one cigarette after another, drinking one cocktail after another, and complaining of boredom. I've also watched people in the midst of the noisy city smiling and laughing, surrounded by the abrasive sounds and people that only the city can manufacture. I've heard them whistle and sing, and I've recognized that they were at peace in the midst of confusion.

The difference? Jesus Christ, the "Prince of Peace."

Christ Our Peace

When you think of Jesus Christ as "Prince of Peace," you immediately think of his character. Jesus was a man of peace. You see this as you watch him in the different circumstances of life. He was able to fall asleep in the ship in the midst of a storm so threatening that even his fishermen disciples were terrified. He looked at over five thousand hungry people and assured his worried disciples that he knew what he would do. The professional mourners at the home of Jairus laughed in his face when he told them the little girl was only sleeping, but he calmly entered her room and raised her from the dead. Even the two demoniacs in the graveyard of Gadara didn't frighten him. He is "Prince of Peace," so he was able to bring peace to their divided and distressed hearts. In the Garden, Peter pulled out a sword and declared war, but Jesus calmly faced the mob and peacefully surrendered to the arresting officers, even though he knew that Golgotha lay at the end of the road.

Our Lord's "trial" was a travesty of justice. Yet Jesus calmly moved from judge to judge, and "as a lamb to the slaughter,

61

and as a sheep before its shearers is dumb, so He opened not His mouth" (Isa. 53:7). Pilate marveled at his silence. Most prisoners curse their executors, but Jesus prayed, "Father, forgive them, for they do not know what they do" (Luke 23:34). The women of Jerusalem offered him a narcotic, but he refused it so that he might with a clear mind and controlled will accomplish God's eternal purposes on the cross. Our Lord's peace didn't come from the absence of trouble or the presence of narcotics. It came from the depths of his soul where he fellowshiped with the Father.

Peace and character go together. What we do depends a great deal on what we are. The secret of our Lord's peace was his relationship to his Father. As he led his disciples from the upper room to the Garden, he said, "But that the world may know that I love the Father, and as the Father gave Me commandment, so I do" (John 14:31). He loved the Father, and therefore he trusted the Father. This gave him peace.

Jesus Christ was God manifested in human flesh. But when he was here on earth, he laid aside the independent use of his divine attributes and lived by faith in the Father. Satan tempted him to use his divine powers for himself, but he chose to trust the Father. Jesus lived and served as you and I must live and serve: trusting the Word, praying, depending on the Holy Spirit, and loving and trusting the Father.

Righteousness and peace go together. "The work of righteousness will be peace, and the effect of righteousness quietness and assurance for ever" (Isa. 32:17). Our Lord's first concern wasn't peace; it was righteousness. "Peace at any price!" was a statement never found on his lips. Peace without righteousness would be victory for the forces of the evil one. Jeremiah wept over this kind of false peace: "They have also healed the hurt of My people slightly, saying, 'Peace, peace!' when there is no peace" (Jer. 6:14). During our Lord's trial, the two enemies, Herod and Pilate, were made friends together, but it was a false peace because it wasn't based on righteousness. "'There is no peace,' says my God, 'to the wicked'" (Isa. 57:21).

If peace is the possession of adequate resources, then the building of character must be paramount in our lives, for character is our greatest resource. Whatever else people may have, if they don't have character, they have nothing. Building character is the work of the Holy Spirit of God: "But the fruit of the spirit is love, joy, peace. . . ." (Gal. 5:22). The Spirit wants to transform us to make us more like Jesus Christ. As we become more like him, the fruit of the Spirit is produced in our lives.

We're prone to want God to change our circumstances, but he wants to change our character. We think that peace comes from the outside in, when in reality it comes from the inside out. Our hearts carry in them their own war or peace, depending on who is in control, Christ or self. Jesus Christ brings peace because he is peace. The more we become like him, the more we experience his peace and can share it with others.

Peace with God and Man

Being "Prince of Peace" involves not only his character, but also his cross: "having made peace through the blood of His cross" (Col. 1:20). Because of the cross, we can have peace with God (Rom. 5:1) and can also have peace with one another. Jesus has reconciled "all things to Himself . . . whether things on earth or things in heaven" (Col. 1:20).

This present evil world is falling apart like an old abandoned barn and certainly doesn't need a definition of the word "reconcile." What it needs is a demonstration of reconciliation in the lives of God's people. Reconciliation represents the deepest longings of the human heart: "Bring us together again!"

Human history began with everything in harmony, and then sin entered and separated man from God. Before long man was separated from man as Cain killed Abel. Sin, the great divider and destroyer, moved through the human race until the earth was "filled with violence" (Gen. 6:11). God judged the world and wiped it clean, starting afresh with Noah and his family. But the poison was too deep in man's system, for "the imagination of man's heart is evil from his youth" (Gen. 8:21). It wasn't enough to purge the tree of the bad fruit; something had to be done about the rotten roots.

It took God's Son coming to earth to strike the final deathblow that conquered sin. At Bethlehem he was made flesh and entered the human race. At Calvary he was made sin and bore the iniquity of the human race in his own body. The cross is the great meeting place of sinners and a merciful God: "Mercy and truth have met together; righteousness and peace have kissed" (Ps. 85:10). It took the blood of his cross to make peace between sinners and God, and one result of this peace with God is peace with one another. Once you've settled the war on the inside, you can start to settle the wars on the outside. "For He Himself is our peace," writes Paul (Eph. 2:14). In Jesus Christ, sinners are reconciled to God and people are reconciled to one another.

You can trace this ministry of reconciliation in the Book of Acts. In chapter 8, the Ethiopian treasurer is converted, a son of Ham. In chapter 9, it is Saul of Tarsus who meets Jesus, and he was a son of Shem. In chapter 10, it is Cornelius and his household, Gentile children of Japheth, who believe on Jesus and receive the gift of the Spirit. All of these people became members of the family of God and the walls were broken down. "There is neither Jew nor Greek, there is neither slave nor free, there is neither male nor female; for you are all one in Christ Jesus" (Gal. 3:28).

It isn't by accident that the cross is a plus sign, for it is God's place of reconciliation, God's place of peace.

Peace in His Companionship

Another factor in Christ's ministry as "Prince of Peace" is his companionship. To those who love and trust him, his presence brings peace.

As you read the Gospel records, you can't help but notice that the twelve apostles were often disturbed by one thing or another. You hear them asking, "Who is the greatest?" and "What shall we get?" Unlike their Master, they had unrest and war in their hearts. One day they met a man outside their group who was casting out a demon, and they tried to stop him! When a village refused hospitality to Jesus, the disciples wanted to send fire from heaven! Instead of being peacemakers, so often they were troublemakers. But before we judge them too severely, we'd better look at ourselves. How many times has our presence declared war?

The peace of his companionship is seen especially during those hours just before his arrest and crucifixion. To put it mildly, the disciples were torn apart by grief, confusion, and fear. Jesus had told them that he was leaving them to return to the Father. Then he informed them that one of their number was a traitor. When Peter tried to salvage the situation by affirming his loyalty and courage, a statement that must have heartened the other men, Jesus calmly informed Peter that he, too, would fail by denying the Lord three times! Everything the disciples had trusted was suddenly taken from them. No wonder Jesus said, "Let not your heart be troubled!" (John 14:1).

It was the companionship of the Master that helped to give peace. "Peace I leave with you," he told them, "My peace I give to you; not as the world gives do I give to you. Let not your heart be troubled, neither let it be afraid" (John 14:27). You can go to a drugstore and buy tranquilizers, and perhaps go to a vacation spot and buy rest, but you can't buy peace.

Peace is a gift; peace is a person who is a gift. His companionship brings peace. After those chaotic hours that followed his death, the disciples again met their Lord. He said to them, "Peace be with you!" (John 20:19). Then he showed them his hands and his side, because the gift of peace was purchased at the awful price of his own life. For the Christian, peace is not a shallow emotion based on feelings or circumstances. Peace for the believer is a deep confidence and joy based on the victorious work of Christ on the cross. It took his wounds to bring peace to a wounded world.

The fact that Jesus Christ arose from the dead and returned to the Father makes it possible for us to enjoy his companionship today. In heaven today, Jesus is our High Priest, our Melchizedek, our "king of righteousness . . . king of peace" (Heb. 7:1–3). At the cross, righteousness and peace kissed each other; on the throne, righteousness and peace reign through Jesus Christ. When he is your companion in life, you experience his peace. "Yea, though I walk through the valley of the shadow of death, I will fear no evil: for You are with me" (Ps. 23:4). "Fear not, for I am with you; be not dismayed, for I am your God" (Isa. 41:10).

As we walk with Christ on the daily path, he gives us his peace through his Word. "These things I have spoken to you, that in Me you may have peace. In the world you will have tribulation; but be of good cheer, I have overcome the world" (John 16:33). The companionship of Christ is not something that we try to manufacture; it's something that we joyfully accept through the Word of God. He still speaks to his own through his Word, and as he speaks we find his peace filling our hearts. "I will hear what God the LORD will speak, for He will speak peace to His people and to His saints" (Ps. 85:8).

We must remember that God doesn't give us his peace so that we may sit back and enjoy it in "spiritual luxury." He gives us his peace so that we might be able to plunge ourselves into the tangled problems of a needy world and share Christ's peace with those who are at war with themselves and with each other. This is what Paul termed "the ministry of reconciliation" (see 2 Cor. 5:14–21). When the "Prince of Peace" reigns in our lives, then the peace of God rules in our hearts (Col. 3:15). This makes us peacemakers in the ministry of reconciliation. Because Jesus is with us, we need not be afraid.

When Paul was experiencing difficulties in Corinth, the Lord came to him and said, "Do not be afraid, but speak, and do not keep silent; for I am with you. . . ." (Acts 18:9–10). When he was arrested in Jerusalem and it looked like his ministry was over, the Lord came to him and said, "Be of good cheer, Paul; for as you have testified for Me in Jerusalem, so you must also bear witness at Rome" (Acts 23:11). At the end of Paul's ministry, as a prisoner in Rome facing death, he wrote to young Timothy, "At my first defense no one stood with me, but all forsook me. . . . But the Lord stood with me and strengthened me. . . ." (2 Tim. 4:16–17). Paul found peace in the companionship of Christ, and so may we.

But companionship must be cultivated. Our Lord doesn't want to be a divine lifeguard who is summoned only in emergencies. He wants to be involved in every aspect of our lives. He walked with Enoch and Abraham, and he wants to walk with us. He talked with Moses and David, and he wants to talk with us. He went into the fiery furnace with the three Hebrew children, and he wants to share our trials with us. "I will dwell in them, and walk among them. I will be their God, and they shall be My people" (2 Cor. 6:16).

67

What God desires from us is single-hearted devotion to him. It means that all we are and have belongs to him to use as he sees fit. "For to me, to live is Christ" is the way Paul described it (Phil. 1:21), and Peter said, "But sanctify Christ as Lord in your hearts. . . ." (1 Peter 3:15 NASB).

Peace on Earth

Our Lord will climax his ministry as "Prince of Peace" at his second coming when he defeats his enemies and establishes his kingdom on earth. He could have brought "peace on earth" as was announced at his birth, but his people said, "We will not have this man to reign over us" (Luke 19:14). The announcement of "peace on earth" was a valid one. God didn't fail; people did.

When the people rejected him, Jesus said, "Do you suppose that I came to give peace on earth? I tell you, not at all, but rather division" (Luke 12:51). He wept over Jerusalem because they were ignorant of the things that made for their peace (Luke 19:41–42). There was no peace on earth, nor could there be, without him who is "Prince of Peace." No wonder the Palm Sunday crowd shouted, "'Blessed is the King who comes in the name of the LORD!' Peace in heaven and glory in the highest!" (Luke 19:38). There was no peace on earth, but thanks to the cross there would be peace in heaven.

The only place you will find peace on earth today is wherever there is a little bit of heaven. There's peace today in heaven, peace purchased by the blood of his cross. There's peace in the hearts of his people who have come to that cross and experienced his salvation. But there will be no peace on earth until he returns and establishes his kingdom. "Of the increase of His government and peace there will be no end, upon the throne of David, and over His kingdom, to order it, and to establish it with judgment and justice from that time forward, even forever. The zeal of the LORD of hosts will perform this" (Isa. 9:7).

It is when the "Prince of Peace" is on his throne that the great promises of peace found in the Prophets will be fulfilled. The lion will lie down with the lamb. The nations will beat their swords into plowshares. Men will study war no more.

Meanwhile, we wait for his coming. And as we wait, we enjoy his peace and we share his peace with a troubled world around us. We love him; we labor for him; we look for him. We long for that day when he shall reign, and when the breathtaking promises of Psalm 72 will be fulfilled: "The mountains will bring peace to the people. . . . He shall come down like rain upon the grass before mowing, like showers that water the earth. In His days the righteous shall flourish, and abundance of peace, until the moon is no more" (vv. 3, 6–7).

Even so, come quickly, Lord Jesus!

PART 2

The Names
of Jesus
from the
New Testament

THE NAZARENE

ome Bible students claim that there are more than seven hundred different names and titles of Jesus Christ recorded in the Bible. Jesus Christ is so great in his person and work that it takes hundreds of names and titles to describe him, and it will take all eternity for us to begin to understand them.

Why should we study the wonderful names of Jesus? For this reason: every name that he wears is a blessing that he shares. The better we understand the names of our Lord Jesus Christ, the better we will know him. The better we know him, the better we'll understand what he's done for us and what he can do for us today. The names of Christ are revelations of his glorious character and his gracious ministry to his own people, and we want to appropriate by faith every blessing that he has for us.

I want to start this series of studies by examining the misunderstood name "Nazarene." "And he [Joseph] came and dwelt in a city called Nazareth, that it might be fulfilled

73

which was spoken by the prophets, 'He shall be called a Nazarene'" (Matt. 2:23).

Understanding the Name

Perhaps the most common name that was used to identify our Lord when he was here on earth was "Jesus of Nazareth" or "Jesus the Nazarene." Jesus was born in Bethlehem of Judea, but the common people didn't identify him with Bethlehem; they identified him with Nazareth in Galilee. Even the religious leaders, who should have known the messianic prophecy in Micah 5:2, identified Jesus with Galilee. "Search and look, for no prophet has arisen out of Galilee" (John 7:52).[1]

It was in Nazareth that Jesus spent his early years (Matt. 2:22–23; Luke 2:39–40, 51), learning Joseph's trade as a carpenter (Mark 6:3). At the age of thirty, when he began his public ministry, Jesus left Nazareth and began to travel throughout the Holy Land ministering to the people. Because he came from Nazareth, Jesus was given the title "Jesus of Nazareth."

According to Matthew, this name was given in fulfillment of "that which was spoken by the prophets." The interesting thing is this: Nazareth is mentioned thirty times in the New Testament, but not once in the Old Testament. And nowhere in the Old Testament do we find a specific prophecy that says, "He shall be called a Nazarene."

As we seek to understand the name "Nazarene," we must not confuse "Nazarene" with "Nazirite" (see Num. 6). The word "Nazirite" means "consecrated by a vow" and refers to people who were set apart by God for a specific time. To be sure, the Lord Jesus Christ was totally separated unto his Father, for he was "holy, harmless, undefiled, separate from sinners" (Heb. 7:26), but the Lord Jesus Christ was not a Nazirite.

Nazirites were not supposed to touch dead bodies (Num. 6:6–9), but Jesus didn't hesitate to identify with the dead. He touched the coffin of the son of the widow of Nain (Luke 7:14), and he tenderly took the hand of the dead daughter of Jairus (Luke 8:54).

Nazirites were not supposed to be identified with the fruit of the vine, but our Lord drank wine. In contrast to John the Baptist, who was a Nazirite (Luke 1:15), the Lord Jesus Christ accepted invitations to dinners, attended wedding feasts, and didn't separate himself from the everyday social life of the people. "The Son of Man came eating and drinking, and they say, 'Look, a glutton and a winebibber'" (Matt. 11:19; see Luke 22:18). So the name "Nazarene" is not the equivalent of "Nazirite," although our Lord Jesus was completely devoted to God.

Many Bible students associate the name "Nazarene" with the Hebrew word *netser,* which means "a branch." In Isaiah 11:1, the Messiah is associated with the title "Branch": "There shall come forth a rod from the stem of Jesse, and a Branch shall grow out of his roots."

The "branch" image isn't difficult to understand. In Old Testament days, it looked as though David's family tree had been "chopped down" (Isa. 10:33–34) and that the future for the kingdom was bleak. Then Jesus was born in Bethlehem into David's family (Matt. 1:1; Luke 1:32), "a root out of a dry ground" (Isa. 53:2), the "Branch" who fulfills the kingdom promises given to David (2 Sam. 7; Luke 1:32–33). Jesus alone is "a Rod from the stem of Jesse, and a Branch . . . out of his roots" (Isa. 11:1). One day Jesus shall reign on the earth and establish the kingdom in glory and power (Isa. 9:6–7).

We have a problem, however, if we connect "Nazarene" with the Hebrew word *netser.* Most of the passages that refer to the Lord Jesus as the "branch" do not use the word *netser*; they use another Hebrew word for "branch." Only in Isaiah 11:1 do we find a "Branch" prophecy about the Lord Jesus using the word *netser*.[2]

It doesn't appear that "Nazarene" comes from *netser*, and it certainly doesn't come from "Nazirite." Then what is the basis for Matthew's prophecy that Messiah "shall be called a Nazarene"?

We must remember the kind of reputation the city of Nazareth had in Jesus' day. When Philip was converted and called his friend Nathanael to come and meet the Lord Jesus, Nathanael said, "Can anything good come out of Nazareth?" (John 1:46). In Jesus' day, Nazareth was a despised and rejected place for several reasons. Nazareth had a mixed population of Jews and Gentiles and was probably more Gentile than Jewish. This didn't please the religious leaders at all. Galilee was called "Galilee of the Gentiles" (Matt. 4:15). The people living in Galilee spoke a rough Aramaic dialect, which explains why the people said to Peter, "Surely you are one of them; for you are a Galilean, and your speech shows it" (Mark 14:70). Galilee was a turbulent place and some of the political rebels of that day made their headquarters in Nazareth.

All in all, Nazareth in Galilee wasn't the kind of place a strict Jew would want to live, but Jesus grew up in Nazareth. Nazareth was, as we would say in America, "across town" or "on the other side of the tracks." So when you called somebody a "Nazarene," you were saying he or she wasn't listed in the social register or in the Who's Who of that day. I think our Lord Jesus was known as a Nazarene because he identified himself with the poor, the outcasts, even the people from Nazareth! "Can anything good come out of Nazareth?" (John 1:46).

Are there specific prophecies in the Old Testament that identify Jesus as being despised and rejected? Yes, there are.

Isaiah wrote that Messiah was "despised and rejected by men; a man of sorrows and acquainted with grief" (Isa. 53:3). In fact, Isaiah 53 is a prophetic description of the humiliation and rejection of the Messiah. Psalm 22 describes his humiliation, especially verses 6–8. Psalm 69 is also a messianic psalm (note vv. 4 and 8–9), and while the psalm records David's suffering, it also describes the reproaches and sufferings of our Lord.

The background of Isaiah 11:1 is the Assyrian invasion of Judah, which occurred during the reign of King Hezekiah (Isa. 37). It was a time of chastening for God's people. At the end of the previous chapter (Isa. 10:33–34), the prophet compared this invasion to the chopping down of a forest, the lopping off of the high haughty trees (Jewish leaders). By the time the kingdom of Judah came to an end with the invasion of the Babylonians (606–586), it looked like the "tree" of Judah was nothing but a stump. But from that stump God would cause a humble shoot, a despised Branch, to grow, and he—the Messiah, Jesus Christ—would bring salvation.

So, instead of quoting one specific prophecy, Matthew referred to the several statements of the Old Testament writers that the Messiah would be despised and rejected, that he would identify himself with the poor and the outcasts of the people, and even die on a cursed cross to save them from their sins.

Applying His Name

Now let's apply the significance of this name to our own lives. What does it mean to you and me today that Jesus Christ was called "a Nazarene"?

The Grace of God

This name speaks to us of the grace of God. When Jesus Christ, the Son of God, came into this world, he didn't identify with Jerusalem (the leading city of religion), or with Rome (the great city of law). Nor did he come to Athens (the most prominent city of philosophy). Where did he go? He went to Nazareth; he identified with people who were despised and rejected, the poor and the needy.

But the remarkable thing is this: the Lord Jesus took that despised name "Nazareth" and glorified it! He was known as "Jesus of Nazareth." Wouldn't you be happy to have your name identified with Jesus? Nazareth, a place despised by many, was glorified by Jesus Christ because he identified himself with it. The sad thing is that the people of Nazareth rejected him (Luke 4:16–30). A prophet is always without honor in his own country and among his own people (see Matt. 13:57).

The name "Nazareth" was honored further when Pilate wrote that title for Jesus and put it on the cross: "Jesus of Nazareth, the King of the Jews" (John 19:19). Can you imagine that—"Nazareth" put up high on the cross! When the people came to the tomb after our Lord's resurrection, the angel said, "You seek Jesus of Nazareth" (Mark 16:6). Can you imagine angels mentioning Nazareth? Jesus made the difference!

Our Lord Jesus himself used the name "Nazareth" when he spoke from heaven to Saul of Tarsus: "I am Jesus of Nazareth" (Acts 22:8). He took the name "Nazareth" and lifted it all the way up to heaven!

No matter where you live, no matter how much you own, no matter how unimportant you may seem to other people, Jesus Christ comes to you where you are. He identifies himself with those who are needy, despised, and rejected. Throughout his earthly ministry, he identified with publicans and sinners, with lepers and sick people—people who were unwanted, abused, ignored, and rejected. Jesus hasn't changed. Though exalted on the throne of heaven, he is still "Jesus of Nazareth" and identifies with common people, needy people, rejected people.

Jesus of Nazareth is still passing by, and by faith you can reach out and say, "Lord Jesus, save me; Lord Jesus, help me—this is my need today."

The Word of God

The name "Nazarene" speaks to us not only of the grace of God, but also of the Word of God. Do you know why the Lord Jesus lived in Nazareth? Because God's Word told him to do so. At least twelve times in his Gospel, Matthew says, "This was done that it might be fulfilled which was written by the prophet."

Why was Jesus born in Bethlehem? Because through the prophet Micah, God said that Bethlehem was to be Messiah's birthplace (Micah 5:2). Do you know why those children were slain in Bethlehem by Herod's soldiers? Because the prophet Jeremiah said it would happen (Jer. 31:15; Matt. 2:17–18). Why did Mary and Joseph take Jesus to live in Nazareth? Because the prophets said he would be called a Nazarene, somebody who was despised and rejected (Matt. 2:19–23). Whatever Jesus did when he was here on earth was in fulfillment of the Word of God.

That encourages me! If you and I will just simply obey the Word of God, we will live in the will of God and accomplish the work of God. We should work where we work because God tells us to. We should do what we do because God tells us to. The name "Nazarene" magnifies the Word of God because it's in the Word of God that we find the will of God revealed.

The Sufferings of Christ

There is a third lesson that comes from this name "Nazarene": We should be identified with the sufferings of Christ. Jesus came to a despised and rejected place; he himself was despised and rejected, and we should share in his reproach. Hebrews 13:13 tells us we should go "outside the camp, bearing his reproach." Don't be afraid to suffer for the Lord Jesus. Don't be ashamed to be identified with him. He wasn't ashamed to be identified with us.

The enemies of Christ called the early Christians "the sect of the Nazarenes" (Acts 24:5). That's quite a title—"the sect of the Nazarenes." These proud people looked down on the Christians and asked, "Who are these people who are identified with Jesus of Nazareth? They can't be very important!" Charles Spurgeon said, "If you follow Christ fully you will be sure to be called by some ill name or other."[3]

Never be ashamed of the Lord Jesus or of his gospel! "For I am not ashamed of the gospel of Christ, for it is the power of God to salvation for everyone who believes. . . ." (Rom. 1:16). We must not be ashamed to take up his cross and follow him. In fact, we should be honored to be identified with Jesus Christ—Jesus of Nazareth, Jesus the Nazarene.

I recall a wealthy businessman visiting a Sunday morning worship service of a church I pastored and after the service saying, "Well, I didn't see anybody important there." He wasn't impressed with God's people! He needed to read 1 Corinthians 1:26–29: "For you see your calling, brethren, that not many wise according to the flesh, not many mighty, not many noble, are called. But God has chosen the foolish things of the world to put to shame the wise, and God has chosen the weak things of the world to put to shame the things which are mighty; and the base things of the world and the things which are despised God has chosen, and the things which are not, to bring to nothing the things that are, that no flesh should glory in His presence."

The grace of God, the Word of God, and the sufferings of Christ—these are all wrapped up in this wonderful name, "Jesus the Nazarene." Let's live by the grace of God, let's obey the Word of God, and let's be very careful that in everything we do we are not ashamed of the Lord Jesus Christ but willingly, yes, gladly bear his reproach.

Nathanael asked, "Can anything good come out of Nazareth?" (John 1:46). Yes, something good did come out of Nazareth—the Lord Jesus Christ, the holy Son of God. He left Nazareth and ministered to needy people. Wherever there were people who were broken and hurt, Jesus was there to heal. Wherever there was sin, he was there to forgive. If you will just open your heart and trust Christ as your Savior, you will be saved by the grace of God. You can then live in obedience to the Word of God. You can then be identified with him in "the fellowship of His sufferings" (Phil. 3:10), unashamed of the Lord Jesus Christ, and living to glorify him.

Jesus of Nazareth is passing by (Luke 18:37). Will you trust him now, before it's too late?

THE PIONEER

Our English word "pioneer" comes from an old French word that means "a foot soldier." The pioneer was the man who went in advance of the main troops and with his buddies opened the way for them to follow, something like our modern infantry. The American poet Walt Whitman wrote:

> Conquering, holding, daring, venturing
> as we go the unknown ways.
> Pioneers! O pioneers!

We who live in modern cities are prone to forget that centuries ago people risked their lives to open the way for others to follow. We are latecomers.

The Word of God tells us that Jesus Christ came to be a pioneer. You may say, "I read my Bible carefully, but I've never noticed that Jesus is called a pioneer." In the Authorized Version, the Greek word *archegos* is twice translated "prince" (Acts 3:15 and 5:31), once translated "captain"

(Heb. 2:10), and "author" (Heb. 12:2). But the meaning is the same: one who takes the lead, who goes before so that others may follow.

The word "pioneer" or "prince" is a Greek word made up of two words which mean "to begin" and "to lead." The word "pioneer" or "prince" really means "someone who starts something, opens the way, and then leads the way so that others might follow." Many Greek students think that the best translation of *archegos* is the word "pioneer."

There is something fascinating about the pioneer days. Many cities have "pioneer days" when they celebrate their founding. We enjoy books and dramas about the pioneer days because there's something challenging about the pioneers. A man with his family goes off into new territory and he opens the way for others to follow. He's a trailblazer. "Him [Christ] God has exalted to His right hand to be Prince and Savior. . . ." (Acts 5:31). Jesus the Pioneer!

The four references to this title "Pioneer" open up for us several different aspects of our Lord's ministry. Remember, every name that Jesus wears is a blessing that he shares. Jesus is the Pioneer and he wants to lead us into challenging new frontiers of spiritual blessing. The tragedy is that too many of us as Christians are making very little progress into new territory. You never stand still in the Christian life; you either move forward or go backward. Like the Jews at Kadesh-Barnea, we must enter new territory for Christ and march forward by faith (Num. 13–14).

Sad to say, some of God's people don't want to move into new territory. They want to keep walking on the same treadmill, going nowhere, like Israel wandering around in the wilderness for forty years. I've heard Christians say, "I enjoy our little church just the way it is. Why do we have to bring in new people?" Why? Because if the church doesn't grow, it dies! If we don't conquer new territory, we have no reason for even existing.

If you want to make progress in your Christian life, then learn what it means to have Jesus Christ as your Pioneer. But what kind of a pioneer is he?

He's the Pioneer of Life

Listen to the apostle Peter as he speaks about the Lord Jesus to the crowd who witnessed the healing of the lame man: "The God of Abraham, Isaac, and Jacob, the God of our fathers, glorified His Servant Jesus, whom you delivered up and denied in the presence of Pilate, when he was determined to let Him go. But you denied the Holy One and the Just, and asked for a murderer to be granted to you, and killed the Prince of life, whom God raised from the dead, of which we are witnesses" (Acts 3:13–15). Peter boldly named their crime: they killed the Pioneer of life!

Most people are more concerned about making a living than making a life. They know the price of everything but the value of nothing. They're merely existing, drifting through life with no goals, no spiritual values, no real life. But the Lord Jesus says to the world, "Look, I'm the Pioneer of life! I want you to walk on the road I opened up that leads to life everlasting. I've opened a new and a living way, and I want to share it with you."

This statement is really a paradox, for how could anybody kill "the Prince of life"? If Jesus is "the Prince of life," then he's the author of life and cannot die. As God, Jesus is the eternal Son; but as man, he could suffer and die just like any human. Had he not died, there could be no life for lost sinners. Jesus said, "I am the way, the truth, and the life" (John 14:6). When you put those three titles together, it says, "I am the true and the living way. I am the way that you can trust. I am the way that gives you life." He is the Pioneer of life.

I think the word "life" is perhaps the best description of what it means to be a Christian. "He who has the Son has life" (1 John 5:12). When you trust Christ as your Savior, you receive eternal life as a gift from God; you receive abundant life as you follow the Pioneer of life wherever he leads you.

This is illustrated so beautifully in Acts 3. Peter and John were on their way to the temple to pray when they saw a man, lame from birth, begging at the Beautiful Gate of the temple. Friends carried him there each day, and there he would ask for alms from the people going to the temple services. When the lame man saw Peter and John, he expected to get something from them.

Peter and John could respond in one of two ways. They couldn't give him any coins because they had no money (v. 6). They could either ignore him, the way most people do when they see beggars, or help him in the power of the Lord. So Peter said to him, "Silver and gold I do not have, but what I do have I give you: In the name of Jesus Christ of Nazareth, rise up and walk" (v. 6). Peter reached out, took him by the right hand, lifted him up, and the man was instantly healed.

Up to that point, this man didn't have much life. He was born a cripple. Spiritually speaking, you and I were born "cripples" because of the fall of our first parents, Adam and Eve. We were born beggars; we brought nothing into this world, and we will take nothing out of this world. This man was a cripple and could not help himself. This crippled beggar could never blaze any pioneer trails. He depended on his friends to carry him where he needed to go.

Then along came two Christians who introduced him to Jesus, and the Lord Jesus Christ became the Pioneer of life to this man. He stood up! He began to leap and walk! He entered into the temple with the disciples "walking, leaping, and praising God" (v. 8). Because the Lord Jesus Christ is the Pioneer of life, he can give life and hope to all who trust in him.

Has Jesus opened the way of life for you? Have you trusted him as your Savior, and are you following him as your Lord? If you are, then you are moving forward on that road of life that he's marked out for you. Psalm 16:11 promises, "You will show me the path of life. . . ." The Lord Jesus Christ opened the way of life that you and I might follow. He is the Pioneer of life.

One other fact should be brought out: Since Christ is the Pioneer of life, his people don't have to worry about death. He went before us into the grave and has conquered death and the fear of death. "Death is swallowed up in victory" (1 Cor. 15:54).

I recall reading about a little boy who was very much afraid of death, as many children are. He was even afraid to go to bed at night, lest he die there. (After all, many people do die in bed.) He was invited by a friend to a children's Bible club and there he heard the story about Jesus. He trusted the Savior and his fear of death disappeared. Excitedly, he said to his mother when he arrived home, "I'm not afraid of death any more! Jesus went into the grave ahead of us and he left a light behind!" Yes, Jesus Christ has "abolished death and brought life and immortality to light through the gospel" (2 Tim. 1:10).

He's the Pioneer of Salvation

Hebrews 2:10 is our key verse: "For it was fitting for Him, for whom are all things and by whom are all things, in bringing many sons to glory, to make the captain [Pioneer] of their salvation perfect through sufferings."

The Book of Hebrews was written to a group of Jewish believers to encourage them to go forward in their Christian life. Because of the sufferings they were experiencing, these believers were tempted to live by sight and not by faith. They knew about the beautiful Jewish temple standing prominently in Jerusalem (Matt. 24:1) and the daily sacrifices offered there on the altar. They knew about the priests who carried on the temple services, and they were proud to belong to the nation of Israel.

But now they were believers in Jesus Christ, and this meant living by faith and not by sight. Because of their sufferings, they were tempted to go back to the old life, to the things that they could see and feel. Little did these persecuted saints realize that within a few years Jerusalem and everything in it would be leveled. There would be no more priesthood, sacrifices, or Jewish religious services.

But what difference would that make to them? They had a High Priest in heaven, even though they couldn't see him (Heb. 4:14–16). They even had a city being prepared for them in heaven (Heb. 11:13–16; 13:14). Why go back to the old sacrifices and the old priesthood on earth when they had the "new and living way" in heaven? (Heb. 10:19–25). These Jewish believers were tempted to go back to the visible and reject the invisible.

According to Hebrews 2:10, Jesus Christ, the Captain of our salvation, was made "perfect through sufferings." Because of the things he suffered on earth, Jesus was prepared for his high priestly ministry in heaven. The word translated "captain" is the word "pioneer." Jesus is the Pioneer of salvation, and he wants us to move ahead and not look back (Luke 9:62) or go back (Heb. 6:1–2). Paul had the same thing in mind when he wrote "forgetting those things which are behind and reaching forward to those things which are ahead" (Phil. 3:13).

The fact that Jesus Christ is the Pioneer of life is a truth that excites me! Many people think salvation is a static experience. They say, "I've trusted Jesus Christ. I've been born again, and that's it!" But salvation involves so much more than just the forgiveness of sins and being born into the family of God! Salvation isn't a parking lot; it's a launching pad. The Lord Jesus Christ is the Pioneer of our salvation, which means there's always something new to learn, experience, and share with others.

The people in Jerusalem who went to the temple and took part in the divine ceremonies were limited in their progress. When they came to the temple, they could go only as far as the altar. They couldn't go into the Holy Place. The Levites and the priests could go into the Holy Place of the temple, but even they could not go into the Holy of Holies. Only the high priest could go into the Holy of Holies, and he did that once a year on the Day of Atonement.

For those Jewish people, there was always a barrier between themselves and God. For those who are Christians, however, nothing stands in the way except our own unwillingness and unbelief. Hebrews 10:19–20 is an invitation that encourages us to come boldly into the Holy of Holies by the new and living way, which Jesus Christ consecrated for us when he died on the cross.

The question I want to ask is this: Is your salvation experience static and boring, or is it exciting? Are you standing still, going backward, or moving ahead into new territory? Then follow the Pioneer of your salvation! As you follow him, salvation becomes a growing and a glowing experience. As you follow him, he takes you through the veil and into the very Holy of Holies. There you fellowship with the living God!

Follow the Pioneer of your salvation!

He's the Pioneer of Faith

Hebrews 12:2 says, "Looking unto Jesus, the author [Pioneer] and finisher of our faith." Jesus is not only the Pioneer of life and the Pioneer of salvation, but he is also the Pioneer of faith. This means that our faith must make progress; we can't stand still. There are degrees of faith: "no faith" (Mark 4:40), "little faith" (Matt. 6:30; 8:26), "great faith" (Matt. 8:10). We need to pray with the apostles, "increase our faith" (Luke 17:5).[1] I wonder what kind of report card I would get if God were to grade me on my faith!

Jesus Christ is the Pioneer of our faith, the "author and finisher of our faith." As the Pioneer, whatever he starts he finishes. That's the beautiful thing about following the Lord Jesus. When you trust his Word, you know he will finish what he starts. "Being confident of this very thing, that He who has begun a good work in you will complete it until the day of Jesus Christ" (Phil. 1:6).

Many people today are hurting, facing difficult problems, and carrying heavy burdens. They're wondering why God has permitted certain painful things to happen to them. But here's the wonderful news: The Pioneer of your faith, the Lord Jesus Christ, wants you to grow and make progress in your Christian life. He wants you to move forward so he can give you new experiences of blessing and enrichment. That's why he permits trials and suffering. He can use these painful experiences to move us forward in the Christian life.

We need not be afraid of the future because Jesus goes before us. He's the Pioneer of life and will guide our path. He's the Pioneer of salvation and gives us new experiences of joy and blessing as we grow. He's the Pioneer of faith who wants us to grow in our faith, become stronger, and claim new territory in the inheritance he's assigned to us.

How do we follow the Pioneer of our salvation? Through the Word of God. The Lord has spoken to us through his Word, and it's important that you and I study the Word, trust the Word, and obey it. Do you read your Bible daily and meditate on what it says? Do you pray daily and claim his promises? Whatever your burden or problem may be, take time to get alone daily with Jesus Christ, the Pioneer of life, the Pioneer of salvation, the Pioneer of faith. If you follow him, you will start to move forward in an exciting new way in your Christian life and testimony.

Peter temporarily slipped back into the old life and denied his Lord three times, but Jesus restored Peter and said to him, "Follow Me" (John 21:19). Peter began to follow the Lord and walked right into the Book of Acts! The Pioneer was guiding him and what a time Peter had as he followed the Lord! Life was exciting and enriching, even if at times it was difficult and painful. There's always something new when you're walking with a pioneer, and Jesus helps us to "walk in newness of life" (Rom. 6:4).

It's very easy for a pioneer to become a settler, but that's not the way the Lord wants us to live. As our Pioneer goes before us preparing the way, his challenge to us is: "Go on to perfection [maturity]!" (Heb. 6:1). The comfortable Christian very soon becomes a conformable Christian (Ps. 1:1; Rom. 12:2), needing the Lord's chastening to get moving again.

The night I graduated from seminary, the commencement ceremonies were held in Orchestra Hall in Chicago. The class hymn was "Lead On, O King Eternal." (I think the school used that hymn for every commencement.) What I didn't know was that Ernest Warburton Shurtleff wrote those words to be sung at his own graduation from seminary in 1887! As he thought about his years of preparation, Shurtleff realized that it would take more than books and lectures to make him a faithful and victorious Christian soldier. But he knew that the Lord went before him, so he wrote:

Lead on, O King eternal,
We follow not with fears;
For gladness breaks like morning
Where'er your face appears;
Your cross is lifted o'er us,
We journey in its light;
The crown awaits the conquest;
Lead on, O God of might.

The future is your friend when Jesus is leading you. Follow the Pioneer wherever he goes!

THE CARPENTER

hen our Lord was ministering here on earth, he talked about many different vocations. He said, "Behold, a sower went out to sow" (Matt. 13:3); but Jesus was not a farmer. He said, "I am the good shepherd" (John 10:14); but when our Lord was here on earth, he didn't care for literal sheep. Before he was baptized by John the Baptist and began his public ministry, do you know what our Lord's vocation was? He was a carpenter.

> Then He went out from there and came to His own country, and His disciples followed Him. And when the Sabbath had come, He began to teach in the synagogue. And many hearing Him were astonished, saying, "Where did this Man get these things? And what wisdom is this which is given to Him, that such mighty works are performed by His hands! Is this not the carpenter, the Son of Mary, and brother of James, Joses, Judas, and Simon? And are not His sisters here with us?" And they were offended at Him. But Jesus said to them, "A prophet is not without honor

except in his own country, among his own relatives, and in his own house." Now He could do no mighty work there, except that He laid His hands upon a few sick people and healed them. And He marveled because of their unbelief. Then He went about the villages in a circuit, teaching. (Mark 6:1–6)

When Jesus came to earth, why did he choose the vocation of a carpenter? Certainly he was a teacher and a healer, but he taught and healed after he had first worked for many years as a carpenter. During the years that he lived in Nazareth, he learned the trade from Joseph and day after day worked with his tools at the bench.

Let me suggest some reasons why Jesus was a carpenter.

He Was Born into a Carpenter's Home

Jesus was born into a carpenter's home, for Joseph, his foster father, was a carpenter. In Matthew 13:55 we read, "Is this not the carpenter's son?" Contrary to what most of the Jewish people expected, their Messiah was born into a carpenter's home. They thought that their Messiah would come as a great king, born in a splendid palace. But he was born into the humble home of a carpenter. The people wanted their Messiah to be a great soldier, a conqueror who would deliver them from the power of Rome. But Jesus came as a laborer, a servant, a carpenter.

The Old Testament Scriptures predicted that he would come as a servant. In Isaiah 52 and 53, the prophet describes the suffering servant of the Lord, a picture of Jesus Christ. In Philippians 2:5–8, Paul describes Jesus Christ the servant. When our Lord Jesus Christ came into this world, according to Hebrews 10:7, he said, "Behold, I have come . . . to do Your will, O God." Jesus came as a humble servant; he came as a carpenter.

Christ identified himself with the common people, and "the common people heard Him gladly" (Mark 12:37). Years of labor as a carpenter helped him understand their burdens and their needs. He knew the dignity of honest labor. He knew what it was like to work and to be weary. "If you do not teach your son how to work," said the rabbis, "you teach him how to steal." The Jewish people taught their children to work, and even the rabbis had their own vocations. Paul, you will recall, was a tentmaker.

Jesus was a laborer who identified with the working people. In the household of Mary and Joseph, he helped to carry the burdens and meet the needs. The Greeks despised manual labor, and the Romans relegated it to their slaves; but among the Jews, "Six days you shall labor and do all your work" was as important as "Remember the sabbath day, to keep it holy" (Exod. 20:8). They saw work as a sacred responsibility before the Lord who gives men and women the power to get wealth (Deut. 8:18).

Were all of Joseph's customers easy to get along with? Perhaps not, but Jesus was patient with them and served them in love. Did anybody who hired Jesus notice that there was something special about his work? Probably not, but he did his best just the same. After all, he wasn't just serving customers; he was serving his Father in heaven.

He Came to Do Carpenter's Work

Not only was Jesus born into a carpenter's home, but he came to do a carpenter's work. What does a carpenter do? He builds and repairs. I must admit that I don't have that kind of skill. I wish I could pick up the toolbox and go around the house fixing things, but I don't have those skills. Other members of my family do, but not I. Jesus came to do a carpenter's work. He was skilled at building and repairing.

I can imagine people coming to the carpenter shop in Nazareth and bringing Jesus broken tables and chairs, or giving him requests for new pieces of furniture or plows. Perhaps the children came with their broken toys, and Jesus gladly fixed them. He spent those "hidden years" in Nazareth building and repairing.

But building was nothing new to the Lord Jesus, for before he came to earth he had built the universe, and it's still functioning right on schedule. "All things were made through Him, and without Him nothing was made that was made" (John 1:3). "For by Him all things were created that are in heaven and that are on earth, visible and invisible, whether thrones or dominions or principalities or powers. All things were created through Him and for Him. And He is before all things, and in Him all things consist [hold together]" (Col. 1:16–17).

But Jesus hasn't abandoned his vocation as the builder, for today he is building his church (Matt. 16:18). If I understand the New Testament correctly, the church is made up of all those who have trusted Jesus Christ as their Savior and belong to him. God's children are living stones in the temple that Christ is building (1 Peter 2:5), "being built together for a dwelling place of God in the Spirit" (Eph. 2:22). Every time a sinner trusts the Savior, a new living stone is added to the temple. Jesus Christ built the universe, and he is building his church. Are you a part of this marvelous temple that he is building?

Jesus Christ is the builder, but Satan is the destroyer. Jesus said, "The thief does not come except to steal, and to kill, and to destroy" (John 10:10). Satan is that thief. Satan is called "Abaddon" and "Apollyon" (Rev. 9:11), both of which mean "destruction." Sin is a great destroyer, and Satan tempts people into sin. Sin destroys bodies, homes, churches, and nations; but Jesus Christ came to build, not to destroy. He offers eternal life and abundant life to all who will trust him.

Jesus the Carpenter is building his people a home in heaven. "I go to prepare a place for you. And if I go and prepare a place for you, I will come again and receive you to Myself. . . ." (John 14:2–3). The wonderful thing about knowing Jesus as your Savior is that you know where you're going. You may not know how long it will take you to get there, but that doesn't matter. We don't know if Jesus will return and take us to glory or if we'll go to sleep in Jesus and wake up in heaven. This the Lord hasn't told us. But he has assured us that he's building a home for us in heaven, and that promise, to me, is a great encouragement. The Carpenter who built the universe, the Carpenter who is building his church, is also building for his people a home in heaven.

But he's also building our lives, if we yield to him. Right now your life is either being built up by the Lord Jesus or being torn down by the devil. There is no middle ground. We never stand still in the Christian life; we're either being built up or being torn down. The greatest destroyer in all the universe is sin, but Jesus Christ came to put away sin and to begin the wonderful process of building our lives.

The people saw Jesus perform miracles and said, "Such mighty works are performed by His hands!" (Mark 6:2). But Mark 6:5 says, "Now He could do no mighty work there, except that He laid His hands on a few sick people and healed them." Why was Jesus unable to do anything special for the people in Nazareth? "And He marveled because of their unbelief" (Mark 6:6). The Lord Jesus Christ wants to build your life, and he will if you will trust him.

One of the key word's in Paul's vocabulary was "edify," which means "to build up." As God's people, we're either working with Jesus to build ourselves, others, and his church, or we're working with the devil to tear things down. It takes

95

patience and skill to build, but anybody, even a child, can destroy. A group of common laborers can destroy in a few days what it took an architect and contractor years to erect. "Let all things be done for edification" (1 Cor. 14:26). But the motive for edification is love. "Knowledge puffs up, but love edifies" (1 Cor. 8:1). God bestows gifts on his people so that they will exercise those gifts in the church "for the equipping of the saints for the work of ministry, for the edifying of the body of Christ" (Eph. 4:12). When "every part does its share," this "causes growth of the body for the edifying of itself in love" (Eph. 4:16).

What a privilege we have to work with the Carpenter and assist in the building of his church!

He Uses a Carpenter's Methods

There is a third reason why the Lord Jesus was a carpenter. Not only was he born in a carpenter's home and came to do a carpenter's work, but he also uses a carpenter's methods. A carpenter looks at a piece of wood and sees the potential in it. Then he forms a plan and patiently goes to work to transform that wood into something useful and beautiful.

You and I might not see the potential in a piece of wood, but the carpenter can see it. No doubt in his youth our Lord went out with Joseph and chose a tree because he saw real potential in it.

God looks at you and says, "I see potential in you." You may look at yourself in the mirror and say, "I can never become anything. I can never do anything." Yes, you can! Jesus looked at Simon one day and said, "I know who you are. You are Simon, but I'm going to call you Peter, a rock" (see John 1:42). Peter's friends may have laughed at this because they didn't see much in Peter that was rocklike.

But Jesus saw the potential in Peter, and that potential was realized.

Our Lord saw the potential in the fishermen he called to follow him, in Levi the tax collector, and in the publicans and sinners who gathered to hear him. When Saul of Tarsus was ravaging the church, Jesus saw his potential and called him to become Paul the apostle. Paul gave up on John Mark (Acts 15:36–41), but Jesus saw the potential in him and eventually made him an effective servant (2 Tim. 4:11).

Jesus sees the potential in you and me and can make us what he wants us to be, if we will let him. Like Moses (Exod. 3–4) and Jeremiah (Jer. 1), we may argue with him about our competence, but he knows what he's doing. "And who is sufficient for these things?" asked Paul (2 Cor. 2:16); then he answered his own question by writing, "Not that we are sufficient of ourselves . . . but our sufficiency is from God who also made us sufficient as ministers of the new covenant. . . ." (2 Cor. 3:5–6).

The Lord follows a carpenter's methods: he sees the potential that is in the material; he has a plan; and he sees the work through to the end. He knows what he wants you to do and he is able to accomplish his purposes if we will yield to him and let him have his way. He knows what he wants you to become. You don't have to drift through life, wondering what to do next. Just turn yourself over to the Carpenter and let him fulfill his plan for you. "For we are His workmanship [manufactured product], created in Christ Jesus for good works, which God prepared beforehand that we should walk in them" (Eph. 2:10).

Jesus the Carpenter is so patient! He takes such great pains with what he does! He knows what tools to use and how to use them. He knows when I have to be planed and sanded, and he knows when I'm ready to be polished. Sometimes he uses the Word of God to correct what's wrong in our lives; other times he uses fellow Christians to rebuke

97

us, encourage us, and polish us. The Lord Jesus follows a carpenter's methods, and he always finishes what he starts. He never leaves a job half done. Our responsibility is to surrender to him and let him follow his plan.

He Died a Carpenter's Death

Jesus was born into a carpenter's home. He came to do a carpenter's work—building and repairing. He follows a carpenter's methods. But he also died a carpenter's death. He wasn't stoned to death; he was nailed to a tree. I wonder how many times our Lord Jesus had carried trees back to the carpenter's shop and trimmed them, cured the wood, cut the boards and planed them, and then made from that wood some useful implement.

One day they took the Lord Jesus, and with hammers and nails—the kind of tools that he had used in the carpenter's shop—the Roman soldiers nailed him to a tree. Peter wrote: "Who Himself bore our sins in His own body on the tree" (1 Peter 2:24). Of course, it was not the nails that held him to that cross; it was his love for lost sinners and his obedience to the Father's will. He died a carpenter's death and was nailed to a tree.

Do you know why he died that kind of a death? The Old Testament law declared, "For he who is hanged [on a tree] is accursed" (Deut. 21:23). When Jesus died on that tree, he bore the awful curse of the law for us so that we might be saved. "Christ has redeemed us from the curse of the law, having become a curse for us, (for it is written, 'Cursed is everyone who hangs on a tree')" (Gal. 3:13).

Whenever you think of Jesus Christ the Carpenter, just remember the price that he paid to save us from hell and to make something out of our lives. Every saved person is a "brand plucked from the fire" (Zech. 3:2). Just as a carpenter has to cleanse each piece of wood and cut away all that's ugly and not needed, so Jesus Christ, in dying for us, cleansed us from our sins. When you trust him, he saves you; then he begins to work in your life to make you what you ought to be.

Whose hands are forming your life? Is Satan destroying you or is Jesus shaping you? Perhaps you're saying, "I'm a self-made man" or "I'm a self-made woman!" But nobody can amount to much whose life is "self-made." Of ourselves and in ourselves, we don't have what it takes to make a success out of life in the eyes of God. But when you put your life into the hands of the Lord Jesus, the wonderful Carpenter, he will save you and make something out of you.

Yes, Jesus Christ is the Carpenter. He was born into a carpenter's home, so he identifies with us. He came to do a carpenter's work—to build and repair our lives so that we become things of beauty for his glory. He follows a carpenter's methods, patiently fulfilling the plan that he has for us. And in order to make all of this possible, he died a carpenter's death on a cruel cross.

The hands that shape our lives are wounded hands, loving hands, skilled hands, powerful hands; so we don't have to be afraid. His hands can do anything, but what he does for us is limited by our faith. "According to your faith let it be to you" (Matt. 9:29).

He is able. Are we willing?

Our Surety

One of the most important titles of our Lord Jesus is used only once in the Scriptures, and yet its message permeates all of the Bible. It's found in Hebrews 7:22: "By so much more Jesus has become a surety of a better covenant."

That verse is right in the middle of a rather complex chapter about the present heavenly priesthood of Jesus Christ. Today the Lord Jesus Christ is our High Priest in heaven, interceding for his people. The Old Testament priests died and therefore were unable to continue in their ministry, but this is not so with our High Priest. Jesus lives forever and therefore can minister forever. Hebrews 7:24 states, "But He [Jesus], because He continues forever, has an unchangeable priesthood." This is why he is called the believer's "surety": he will live forever to represent us before the throne of God.

Someone who becomes "surety" for another assumes a responsibility for that person, usually with reference to pay-ing a debt. In many cities, wherever there's a courthouse, you'll find a jail, and near that jail you'll usually find the offices of the bondsmen, the people who sell the bail bonds. These men are available to become surety for the people who have to post bond. The judge orders the accused to post a $10,000 bond, so the bondsman will post the bond and the accused will pay him for his services. The bondsman becomes surety for the accused, assuring the court that the accused will appear at the trial. The Greek word means "to make a pledge, to offer security, to undertake an obligation for another."

However, suretyship is different from mediation. Jesus Christ is also our mediator (Heb. 8:6; 9:15; 12:24), but that's a different ministry from being our surety. A mediator gets two estranged parties together, but the mediator isn't obligated to pay a price in order to do so. The surety is the one who is the guarantee that the price will be paid; he is the security. Our Lord Jesus Christ today is our surety in heaven.

We want to examine three different aspects of the truth of Christ's suretyship: *explanation*—what it means; *illustration*—where we find it in Scripture; and *application*—what it means to believers today.

The Explanation of Suretyship

Often in the Book of Proverbs Solomon warns about becoming surety for somebody, not even a friend and especially not a stranger. "My son, if you become surety for your friend, if you have shaken hands in pledge for a stranger, you are snared by the words of your own mouth; you are taken by the words of your mouth. So do this, my son, and deliver yourself; for you have come into the hand of your friend: go and humble yourself; plead with your friend. Give

101

no sleep to your eyes, nor slumber to your eyelids. Deliver yourself like a gazelle from the hand of the hunter, and like a bird from the hand of the fowler" (Prov. 6:1–5).

When I was in pastoral ministry, a young man I had led to Christ came to me for help in a matter of "surety." In his preconversion days, Harry had signed a note for a friend. Now the "friend" had suddenly left town and couldn't be located. I showed Harry what Solomon wrote about the matter, and all he said was, "I guess when you're lost, you don't know those things." But it also gave me an opportunity to remind Harry of what Jesus Christ had done for him when he became our surety.

We owed God a debt we couldn't pay. We had broken his law, defied his will, wasted his gifts, and broken his heart; we were bankrupt. But Jesus Christ came to this earth to save bankrupt sinners like us. In fact, he became poor for us. "For you know the grace of our Lord Jesus Christ, that though He was rich, yet for your sakes He became poor, that you through His poverty might become rich" (2 Cor. 8:9).

Jesus became poor in his birth, exchanging the glories of heaven for the sufferings of earth. He became poor in his life, and he was especially poor in his death. He became the poorest of the poor that he might make us the richest of the rich.

On the cross Jesus paid the debt that I couldn't pay. When I trusted him, he freely forgave me that debt and became my surety. As long as Jesus lives—and that will be forever—he guarantees my salvation. As my surety, he assures me that I cannot be lost. "Therefore He is also able to save to the uttermost [forever, completely] those who come to God through Him, since He always lives to make intercession for them" (Heb. 7:25).

Too often we read Hebrews 7:25 as though it says that he saves sinners *from* the uttermost, no matter how wicked they have been, and certainly that fact is true. But that's not what Hebrews 7:25 is saying. Yes, Christ can save any sinner *from* the uttermost; but Hebrews 7:25 assures us that he saves sinners "*to* the uttermost." In other words, he saves us completely, and he saves us forever. Why? Because he is our eternal surety.

My salvation is not wrapped up in my good works. My salvation depends on my Savior's finished work on the cross. As long as Jesus Christ is alive, I am saved. How long is he going to live? He will live forever because he has come "according to the power of an endless life" (Heb. 7:16). We are saved to the uttermost because Jesus is our surety.

We need this kind of assurance because Satan accuses the saints before God (Zech. 3:1–5; Rev. 12:10) and sometimes accuses us in our own hearts. He asks God, "Did you see what that Christian did? Did you hear what he just said?"

God the Father says, "Yes, I did."

"If you are a holy God," argues Satan, "you will have to condemn him for that sin."

Then Jesus says, "I am his surety. He cannot be lost because I am the guarantee that he will be saved forever. I paid for all his sins when I died for him. See—behold my wounds!"

The fact that Jesus paid our debt on the cross and stands at the throne as our surety is no excuse for us to sin. Anybody who claims to be a child of God and enjoys deliberately living in sin is simply not a child of God at all. "How shall we who died to sin live any longer in it?" (Rom. 6:2). "Whoever abides in Him does not sin [practice sin]. Whoever sins [practices sin] has neither seen Him nor known Him. Little children, let no one deceive you. He who practices righteousness is righteous, just as He is righteous" (1 John 3:6–7).

When Satan accuses you and your conscience condemns you, confess your sins to the Lord. Remind yourself that Jesus is your surety at the throne of God. He has assumed your debt and paid the full price for your redemption.

Illustrations of Surety

The Bible contains many illustrations of various doctrinal truths, and I've chosen three events that illustrate Christ our surety, two from the Old Testament and one from the New Testament.

Joseph's Brothers

Joseph's brothers hated him and sold him into slavery (see Gen. 37–46), but Joseph ended up in Egypt where God blessed him richly and caused him to become the second ruler in the land. A famine came, and Joseph's brothers had to go down to Egypt to get food. Joseph recognized them, although they didn't recognize him and Joseph set in motion a plan that would lead to his brothers' repentance and reconciliation.

To make sure that all of his brothers would come to Egypt, Joseph did two things: He kept his brother Simeon as a hostage, and he demanded that they bring their youngest brother, Benjamin, with them when they returned to get Simeon (Gen. 42:20). The sons of Jacob returned to Canaan and told their aged father what had happened, and Jacob didn't like it one bit. He refused to let them take Benjamin. After all, Jacob had lost Simeon and Joseph, and he wasn't about to forfeit Benjamin as well (Gen. 42:36–38).

At this point in the drama, Reuben stepped up and offered to take care of Benjamin. "Kill my two sons if I do not bring him [Benjamin] back to you: put him into my hands, and I will bring him back to you" (Gen. 42:37). But Jacob refused his offer, for what good would it do to kill two innocent boys? Would that bring back Joseph and Benjamin and Simeon?

That was all well and good until the famine became worse. Their food from Egypt ran out and Jacob's family started getting hungry. Finally the boys convinced their father that they had to go back to Egypt and take Benjamin with them. Judah stepped up and said something wonderful: "Send the lad with me, and we will arise and go, that we may live and not die, both we and you and also our little ones. I myself will be surety for him; from my hand you shall require him. If I do not bring him back to you and set him before you, then let me bear the blame forever" (Gen. 43:8–9).

Reuben offered to sacrifice his two sons if he didn't bring Benjamin home, but Judah offered *himself* as the surety! What a difference! But that's what the Lord Jesus Christ has done for us. He says to God the Father, "I am surety for these for whom I have died." And God the Father says, "You are a priest forever after the order of Melchizedek, and I will accept you as their surety." Just as Judah was the guarantee to Jacob that Benjamin was safe, so Jesus is the guarantee to his people that they are safe.

Satan and Joshua the High Priest

When the Jewish remnant returned to their land after the Babylonian captivity, they were often in great difficulty because they didn't trust the Lord and obey his Word. God couldn't bless them as he wished because they weren't keeping their part in the covenant he had made with them. Israel was a sinful nation and deserved to be forsaken.

The prophet Zechariah had a vision concerning the sins of the nation and the forgiveness of the Lord (Zech. 3:1–5).

Then he showed me Joshua the high priest standing before the Angel of the LORD, and Satan standing at his right hand to oppose him. And the LORD said to Satan. "The LORD rebuke you, Satan! The LORD who has chosen Jerusalem rebuke you! Is this not a brand plucked from the fire?" Now Joshua was clothed with filthy garments, and was standing before the Angel. Then He answered and spoke to those who stood before Him, saying, "Take away the filthy garments from him." And to him He said, "See, I have removed your iniquity from you, and I will clothe you with rich robes." And I said, "Let them put a clean turban on his head." So they put a clean turban on his head, and they put the clothes on him. And the Angel of the LORD stood by.

The high priest was never to wear filthy garments because he represented the people before the Lord. On his turban was a gold plate which read "HOLINESS TO THE LORD" (Exod. 28:36–37). But when the Jewish remnant sinned against the Lord, they were no longer a holy people, and this was revealed in the condition of Joshua the high priest. No wonder Satan was able to accuse him before God!

But Joshua had a surety at the holy throne of God. It was Jesus Christ, who here is called the Angel of the Lord. Satan stood at Joshua's right hand to accuse him, but Jesus stood at God's right hand to act as surety for the high priest! On the basis of that suretyship, God could forgive the people, cleanse their high priest, and give them a new beginning. It's the Old Testament version of 1 John 1:9.

Jesus has promised to be the surety for his people, and he will never disappoint us. We are saved and safe as long as he is alive, and that will be forever. He paid the price for our salvation and carried those wounds with him to glory.

> There for me the Savior stands,
> Holding forth His wounded hands;
> God is love! I know, I feel,
> Jesus weeps and loves me still.
> (Charles Wesley)

Paul and Onesimus

This is a New Testament picture of the beautiful truth of Christ's suretyship. The story is found in a little letter that Paul wrote to his friend Philemon, a man Paul had led to faith in Christ. Philemon lived in Colosse and had a slave whose name was Onesimus. Onesimus robbed his master and fled to Rome, but by the providence of God he came in contact with Paul and was converted to Christ.

Paul wanted to keep Onesimus in Rome to assist him in his ministry, but he knew he had to send Onesimus back to Philemon so he could make things right with his master. Knowing that Philemon had complete authority over his servant, Paul wrote this letter to prepare the way for Onesimus's return. In this letter, Paul offered to be surety for Onesimus.

> If then you count me as a partner, receive him as you would me. But if he has wronged you or owes anything, put that on my account. I, Paul, am writing with my own hand. I will repay. . . . (Philem. 1:17–19)

Paul said, "I will be surety for Onesimus. I will stand for him. When you look at Onesimus, remember that you are looking at Paul. I will pay his debt."

The Lord Jesus Christ is our surety in heaven. He says to God the Father, "If they owe you anything, I have paid it. Receive them the way you would receive me." By his grace, we have been made "accepted in the Beloved" (Eph. 1:6).

The Application of This Truth

Now let's look at this truth by way of application. What does it mean to God's children today that Jesus Christ is our surety in heaven?

God's Assurance

The suretyship of Jesus is the assurance that God will keep his salvation covenant with his people. God has made a covenant of grace with us through the Lord Jesus Christ. "By so much more Jesus has become a surety of a better covenant" (Heb. 7:22). Salvation isn't the result of some kind of an agreement between sinners and God. It's the result of an eternal covenant between the Father, the Son, and the Spirit. Because of this eternal covenant, salvation involves all three Persons in the Godhead (Eph. 1:3–14; 1 Peter 1:2).

The people to whom the Book of Hebrews was written were tempted to trust in their temple, their ceremonies, their priests, and their sacrifices—the things that belonged to the old covenant. The writer said, "No, you don't need to look back. Jesus Christ is all you need. He is everything. He is your hope, he is your Savior, he is your Lord, and he is your surety." Because the Jewish high priest died, he couldn't be the surety of anything eternal; but Jesus Christ lives forever and is God's assurance to us that his covenant is secure.

We know that God keeps his covenant because God cannot lie (Titus 1:2) and can never do anything that's wrong. But to give us extra assurance that our salvation is secure, he says to us, "My Son is the surety. As long as he is alive, the covenant is secure."

Our Assurance

Christ is our assurance to God. We make promises to God that we don't always keep. Jesus Christ is our assurance to God. We can't keep ourselves saved any more than we could save ourselves to begin with! But Jesus Christ represents us at the throne of God, saying to God the Father, "I am their surety. Whatever they owe you, I have paid. Receive them as you would receive me, because they are my children."

Because of this, we Christians have the wonderful assurance that we cannot lose our salvation. We have a High

Priest in heaven who lives forever. He stands before the throne of God as the guarantee—the pledge, the security—for our salvation. He is our surety forever.

This truth should never make us careless. God doesn't give us assurance to make us careless. Anyone who is truly born again wants to live a godly life. That's why Jesus is interceding in heaven for us today. We can come to him at any time and know we are accepted. We can come to him with any need and know that he will hear and answer.

Just as Judah said to his father, "I will be surety for the lad and will not come home without him," so Jesus Christ says of us, "I am your surety, and you're going to come home with me. I'm building a home for you, and you will live there forever because I am your surety."

"Therefore He is also able to save to the uttermost those who come to God through him, since He always lives to make intercession for them" (Heb. 7:25). The ever living High Priest is our everlasting surety, the surety of a better covenant, a covenant that will never fail.

Alpha and Omega

We're learning in these studies that every name or title that Jesus wears is a blessing that he shares. The better we know him, the better he's able to bless us and make us what he wants us to be. One of the best ways to get to know him is to study his names and titles in Scripture.

Our Lord said, "And behold, I am coming quickly, and My reward is with Me, to give to everyone according to his work. I am the Alpha and the Omega, the Beginning and the End, the First and the Last" (Rev. 22:12–13).

"Alpha and Omega" are the first and last letters of the Greek alphabet. In fact, the English word "alphabet" comes from the first two letters of the Greek alphabet, "alpha" and "beta." When he calls himself "Alpha and Omega," Jesus declares that he is the first and the last, the beginning and the ending. What truths do we learn about the Lord Jesus Christ from this name "Alpha and Omega"?

Jesus Christ Is Eternal God

Jesus Christ is the beginning and Jesus Christ is the ending; he is the first and he is the last. This means that Jesus Christ is eternal God.

If I said to you, "I am Alpha and Omega," you would shake your head and reply, "You're confused; you're not thinking straight." But when Jesus Christ says, "I am Alpha and Omega, I am the First and the Last, the Beginning and the End," he has the right to say it because he is eternal God.

In Isaiah 41:4, Jehovah God declares, "I, the LORD, am the first, and with the last I am He." This same declaration is repeated in Isaiah 44:6 and Isaiah 48:12. In other words, the Jehovah of the Old Testament is the Jesus of the New Testament. Because the title "Alpha and Omega" is applied to God, this means that Jesus Christ is eternal God. Our Lord Himself said in John 8:58, "Before Abraham was, I AM." In Colossians 1:17 we are told, "He is before all things."

As you page through the Book of Hebrews, you will find the word "forever" repeated several times. Hebrews was written to people who wanted to hold on to the past—their holy temple, their holy city, their holy priesthood, and their holy sacrifices; but these things were about to pass away. In fact, a few years after the Book of Hebrews was written, Jerusalem and the temple and the Jewish religious system were completely destroyed. There would be no more altar, priesthood, or sacrifices. So why hold on to the things that will not last when you can build your life on the things that will endure forever?

In Hebrews 1:8 we're told that Christ's throne is forever. No monarch on earth ever had an eternal throne, but Jesus Christ has a throne forever. We read in Hebrews 5:6: "You are a priest forever. . . ." The Old Testament priests died and had to be replaced, but not so with the Lord Jesus.

Hebrews 10:14 states, "For by one offering He has perfected forever those who are being sanctified." In other words, we have a perfect salvation forever through faith in Jesus Christ. Hebrews 13:8 says, "Jesus Christ is the same yesterday, today, and forever." Jesus Christ can't change because he is eternal God. He can't change for the better because he's already perfect; he certainly can't change for the worse because he's holy. The name "Alpha and Omega" declares that Jesus of Nazareth is eternal God.

If you have never trusted Jesus Christ as your Savior, then you have nothing eternal except eternal judgment (2 Thess. 1:9). Our Lord said, "If you do not believe that I am He, you will die in your sins" (John 8:24). Have you tied your life to that which is eternal, or are you building your life on the changing, shifting things in this world? Nothing in this world is going to last. Only God is eternal. When you trust Jesus Christ, you receive eternal salvation.

Jesus Christ Reveals God to Us

A second truth that comes from this wonderful name is that the ministry of Christ is to reveal God to us. What do you do with the letters of the alphabet? You use them to build words; and through words, you communicate with people. Jesus Christ is the Word. "In the beginning was the Word, and the Word was with God, and the Word was God. He was in the beginning with God" (John 1:1–2). "And the Word became flesh and dwelt among us, and we beheld His glory. . . ." (John 1:14). The Lord Jesus Christ is God's eternal Word, revealing the Father to us.

Once again, we go to the Book of Hebrews. One of the major themes of Hebrews is that God has spoken and people must decide what they will do with what he has said. The Epistle to the Hebrews begins, "God, who at various times and in various ways spoke in time past to the fathers by the prophets, has in these last days spoken to us by His Son. . . ." (1:1–2). Toward the end of the Book of Hebrews, it says, "See that you do not refuse Him who speaks. . . ." (12:25). In other words, the major question everybody must answer is: What will you do with the Word of God?

Because Jesus Christ is Alpha and Omega, he is the alphabet of God's revelation to us. From the alphabet of God's revelation, Jesus gives us the Word. If you want to understand God, you have to know Jesus Christ. Many people say, "I get so much truth about God from walking in the woods." You can learn some things about God from nature, but you can't get the full revelation of God apart from Jesus Christ. Others say, "I love to sit and look at a beautiful sunset; it tells me so much about God." But you will learn much more about God by reading the Bible and listening to his Son, Jesus Christ.

God has spoken to us in Jesus Christ, and Jesus Christ is God's last word. Nothing will replace what God has said to us through his Son. If you want to know God, you have to come to Jesus Christ. Jesus Christ is Alpha and Omega; his ministry is the ministry of revelation. He reveals God to us.

During the Last Supper, before Jesus went out to be arrested and then crucified, the apostle Philip said, "Lord, show us the Father, and it is sufficient for us" (John 14:8). Jesus replied, "Have I been with you so long, and yet you have not known Me, Philip? He who has seen Me has seen the Father. . . ." (v. 9). Jesus is Alpha and Omega, the alphabet of God's grace, revealing to us the heart and mind of the Father so that we might know God and have eternal life.

Jesus Christ Is Sufficient

The third truth found in this name "Alpha and Omega" is not only that Jesus is eternal God and reveals the Father to us, but also that he is sufficient for every need that we

113

have. We might say of a wealthy man, "He has everything from A to Z." Well, the Greeks would say, "He has everything from alpha to omega." When Jesus says he is Alpha and Omega, he is saying, "I am sufficient for everything; nothing is missing; I am all that you need."

In the Epistle to the Colossians, at least twenty-three times Paul uses the word "all." We read in Colossians 1:16: "For by Him all things were created"; and verse 17 says of Christ, "And He is before all things, and in Him all things consist [hold together]." We read in verse 18 "that in all things He may have the preeminence." Verse 19 says, "For it pleased the Father that in Him all the fullness should dwell." Colossians 2:3 states that in Christ "are hidden all the treasures of wisdom and knowledge." Colossians 2:9 says of Jesus, "For in Him dwells all the fullness of the Godhead bodily."

You may ask, "What does that mean to me?" Colossians 2:10 tells us what it means: "And you are complete in Him." Because Jesus is Alpha and Omega, he is fully sufficient in everything; because we are in him, we share his sufficiency. When we were born again, we were born with everything we will ever need for life and godliness (2 Peter 1:3).

Did you know that when you trusted Christ as your Savior, you were introduced to eternal sufficiency? Everything you ever need you can get from Jesus Christ. He comes to you and says, "What is it you need? Just spell it out to me. I am Alpha and Omega and I am completely adequate for every situation and sufficient for every need." That's what the grace of God is all about! "And my God shall supply all your need according to His riches in glory by Christ Jesus" (Phil. 4:19).

You may be facing a difficult situation and feel totally inadequate to handle the demands before you. If you know Jesus Christ as your Savior, you can draw upon his sufficiency. Whatever your need is today, he can make you adequate to meet it. "I can do all things through Christ who strengthens me" (Phil. 4:13).

Jesus Christ Is Victorious

There is a fourth lesson in this title. "Alpha and Omega"
means that whatever Jesus starts, he finishes. He is victorious and successful in all that he does.

I confess that I have in my files sermon outlines that I've
never finished and book manuscripts that I have begun to
write but have never completed. There are books in my
library that I started to read but never completed. No doubt
you have some "unfinished business" in your office or work-
shop or garage, but Jesus Christ finishes everything he
starts.

The Book of the Revelation reveals this truth to us. Let
me list for you some of the great "completions" in Revelation
that had their beginning in Genesis.

Genesis	Revelation
The old heavens and earth	The new heaven and earth
Adam gets a bride	Christ gets his Bride
Babylon is built	Babylon is destroyed
Satan begins his career	Satan cast into hell
Man cast out of Paradise	Believers enter paradise
Sin and death enter the scene	No more sin or death

I could go on, but I'm sure you get the message. The Book
of Revelation is the completion of the Book of Genesis,
and it assures us that what God starts in his great program
of redemption he will finish. Jesus is Alpha and Omega.

But it's also true that what God starts in our lives he will
surely finish. Sometimes it looks like God has forgotten us
or forsaken us, but we know this isn't true. Joseph may have
felt abandoned in Egypt, but God finished what he started
and made a great man out of him. In some of his "exile

115

psalms," David asks whether God will ever keep his promises and make him king, but not one promise of God failed. David did become king.

Be encouraged today! Christ is the Alpha and the Omega, the beginning and the end, the first and the last. He cannot fail. What he starts he finishes. Our task is to keep "looking unto Jesus, the author and finisher of our faith. . . ." (Heb. 12:2). Paul reminds us that "He who has begun a good work in you will complete it until the day of Jesus Christ" (Phil. 1:6).

"Alpha and Omega" are names that declare that Jesus Christ is eternal God. These names remind us of his ministry, the living Word who reveals the living God to us. As Alpha and Omega, Jesus Christ lacks nothing, and his sufficiency is available to all of his people. Finally, these names tell of his victory, the fact that he finishes what he begins. We need never be discouraged because he is the beginning and the ending, the first and the last.

> Breathe, O breathe, Thy loving Spirit
> Into every troubled breast!
> Let us all in Thee inherit,
> Let us find that second rest.
> Take away our bent to sinning,
> Alpha and Omega be;
> End of faith as its beginning,
> Set our hearts at liberty.
> (Charles Wesley)

I close with this suggestion: start and end each day by meeting with Jesus Christ. Let him be the Alpha of each morning and the Omega of each night. If Jesus Christ is the Alpha, the key that opens the day, and the Omega, the key that locks the day, then you will abide in him all the day and enjoy his help and blessing.

Whenever you begin a new project, no matter how small it may seem, be sure that Jesus is at the beginning and that you are doing his will. And when the project is ended, thank him for his help and let him be the Omega. Any project or plan that can't have Jesus as Alpha and Omega is suspect and out of the will of God.

Let him be the Alpha and Omega of your life!

The Lamb

One of the prominent names of the Lord Jesus Christ in the Bible is "the Lamb." From the beginning of the Bible to the end, we find Jesus Christ presented as the Lamb. In fact, in the Book of the Revelation, Jesus is called "the Lamb" at least twenty-eight times!

We want to consider four phrases in the Bible that summarize what the Word of God has to say about Jesus Christ the Lamb.

"Where Is the Lamb?"

Abraham and Isaac

The first phrase is a question found in Genesis 22:7. It's the question Isaac asked his father Abraham as they walked together up the mountain: "Look, the fire and the wood, but where is the lamb for a burnt offering?"

God had instructed Abraham to take his beloved son Isaac, his only son, to Mount Moriah and there offer him to the Lord as a burnt offering. Isaac was a young man at this time, not a little child, and he was God's special love gift to Abraham and Sarah. His name means "laughter," and he had brought much joy to his parents. But now God was asking Abraham to give back his son, and neither Abraham nor Isaac disobeyed God's command.

Of course, our loving Father in heaven never asks for dead human sacrifices. He wants us to be "living sacrifices" for his glory (Rom. 12:1–2). Throughout the Old Testament, the prophets condemned the Jewish people when they imitated their pagan neighbors by giving their children as sacrifices to idols. God didn't want Isaac's life; he wanted Abraham's heart, just as he wants our hearts today. The Lord wanted to be sure that Abraham was trusting in him and his promises alone and not trusting in Isaac.

"Where is the lamb?" is a question that was asked throughout the Old Testament period as believing people looked forward to the coming of the Redeemer. Abraham's answer was a good one: "My son, God will provide for Himself the lamb for a burnt offering" (Gen. 22:8). When Abraham bound Isaac, placed him on the altar, and was about to kill him, God provided a ram that took Isaac's place; and one day at Calvary, God provided a Lamb who took our place.

"Where is the lamb?" When Isaac asked that important question, the Lamb of God was in heaven, waiting until "the fullness of the time" (Gal. 4:4) when he would come to earth to die for the sins of the world. But in the mind and heart of God the sacrifice was already assured, for Jesus Christ is "the Lamb slain from the foundation of the world" (Rev. 13:8). Calvary was not an afterthought with God.

According to Hebrews 11, the Old Testament saints were saved by faith just as people today are saved by faith (Eph. 2:8–10). We today *look back* by faith to the finished work of Christ on the cross; but the Old Testament saints *looked ahead* to the coming of the Messiah. Abraham, for example, was looking far beyond Mount Moriah when he replied to Isaac's question. Abraham was looking to Mount Calvary.

Jesus said, "Your father Abraham rejoiced to see My day, and he saw it and was glad" (John 8:56). That's why Abraham answered, "God will provide himself a lamb." That Lamb, Jesus Christ, is not only the burnt offering, but he's also the sin offering, the peace offering, and the trespass offering. Jesus Christ, God's perfect Lamb, came and fulfilled all the Old Testament sacrifices when he died for the sins of the world.

The Exodus from Egypt

Centuries later the Israelites went into Egypt, suffered in slavery, and then were delivered by Moses. At the exodus, the lamb again played an important role. In Exodus 12:3–5, Moses instructed the Jewish people concerning Passover: "On the tenth day of this month every man shall take for himself a lamb, according to the house of his fathers, a lamb for a household. And if the household is too small for the lamb, let him and his neighbor next to his house take it according to the number of the persons. . . . Your lamb shall be without blemish. . . ." (Exod. 12:3–5).

That's an interesting sequence: "*a* lamb, *the* lamb, *your* lamb." Our relationship to the lamb must be personal. Is Jesus Christ *your* Lamb, your personal Savior from sin? Can you honestly say, he "loved me and gave Himself for me" (Gal. 2:20, italics mine)?

The Lamb Led to the Slaughter

On Mount Moriah, God provided a ram to die for Isaac, an individual. At Passover, God provided the lamb to die for a household. But the prophet Isaiah announced that one day the Lamb would die for the nation: "For the transgressions of My people He was stricken" (Isa. 53:8). The

Jewish high priest Caiaphas had this in mind when he said, "Nor do you consider that it is expedient for us that one man should die for the people, and not that the whole nation should perish" (John 11:50). Isaiah 53 is one of the most important messianic chapters in the Old Testament. It describes the humble birth of the Messiah (vv. 1–2), his life of rejection and sorrow (v. 3), and then his sacrificial death for the sins of the people (vv. 4–11). Jesus could have commanded the hosts of heaven to deliver him, yet he willingly "was led as a lamb to the slaughter. . . ." (v. 7).

Isaiah makes it clear that our Lord's death was *substitutionary*. He didn't die for his own sins, for he had none, but for your sin and mine. "But He was wounded for our transgressions, He was bruised for our iniquities, the chastisement for our peace was upon Him, and by His stripes we are healed" (v. 5). The emphasis in that verse is on the word "our." The Lord laid on Jesus Christ, his Son, the Lamb of God, the iniquities of us all (v. 6).

"Behold! The Lamb!"

The question Isaac asked his father was answered centuries later by John the Baptist, recorded in John 1:29. John the Baptist pointed to Jesus and said, "Behold! The Lamb of God who takes away the sin of the world!" Every phrase in that important statement tells us something about the Lord Jesus, God's Lamb, and the salvation that he purchased for us on the cross.

Behold!

John pointed to a person the people could see with their own eyes. In previous centuries, the Redeemer was seen as

121

the Angel of the Lord, who occasionally and temporarily visited the people; or he was revealed in the types and ceremonies at the temple and in the sacrifices brought to the altar. Messiah was seen in the words of the prophets as the Suffering Sacrifice and the Glorious King, and the Jewish scholars had a difficult time understanding this contradiction. How could Messiah suffer so ignominiously and yet reign so gloriously?

But now, the promised Lamb was standing there in flesh and blood, and everybody could see him. The tragedy is, they didn't recognize him! "There stands One among you whom you do not know," was John's indictment (John 1:26). "He came to His own, and His own did not receive Him" (John 1:11).

The Lamb

John said, "Behold! *The* Lamb!" (John 1:29, italics mine). Every Passover thousands of lambs were slain by the Jewish people, but not one of them could be called "*the* Lamb." In the regular daily Jewish worship, at least two lambs were killed, one in the morning and one in the evening. Add to these the special sacrifices that were brought by the people, and the special sacrifices for the holy days, and you can well imagine that millions of lambs had been slain from the time of Moses to the time of John the Baptist. But John was specific; he said, "Behold! *The* Lamb!"

Jesus Christ is God's final Lamb, sacrificed once and for all for the sins of the world. "But this Man, after He had offered one sacrifice for sins forever, sat down at the right hand of God" (Heb. 10:12). It isn't possible for the blood of animals to take away human sin (Heb. 10:1–4), and each animal sacrificed under the law of Moses only pointed to the one sacrifice, Jesus Christ, whose blood can wash away our sins.

There was no other good enough
To pay the price of sin;
He only could unlock the gate
Of heaven and let us in.
(Cecil F. Alexander)

The Lamb of God

Furthermore, Jesus Christ is the Lamb of God: "Behold! The Lamb of God!" (John 1:29). It was God who sent his Son ("The Father has sent the Son as Savior of the world"— 1 John 4:14); but when he came, most of the people neither expected him nor welcomed him. Some of the religious leaders said he was sent by the devil, and the religious officials handed him over to Rome to be crucified.

Jesus was sent by God, yet the people didn't want him. So often in Scripture, humanity rejects the gifts of God. The Jews repeatedly fought with Moses and the prophets, even to the point of killing God's messengers to silence them. Jesus was rejected by his own people even though everything about him pointed to the fact that he was sent by God. Even his own relatives didn't understand him. Jesus wasn't man's choice; he was God's choice. "He is despised and rejected by men, a man of sorrows and acquainted with grief" (Isa. 53:3).

Because he was God's Lamb, he was perfect. At Passover, the Israelites had to pen up their lambs and watch them to make sure they were without blemish (Exod. 12:5–6). The Jews were forbidden to bring to the Lord a sacrifice that was not perfect. The Lord Jesus Christ, the Lamb of God, was examined from every side before he went to the cross. The demons admitted that he was the Son of God. Pilate said, "I find no fault in this Man" (Luke 23:4). Even Judas said he had betrayed "innocent blood" (Matt 27:4). The soldier at the cross said, "Truly this was the Son of God" (Matt. 27:54). The Lord Jesus Christ was examined on every side, and they discovered he was "holy, harmless, undefiled" (Heb. 7:26). He was "a lamb without blemish and without spot" (1 Peter 1:19).

Takes away Sin

The blood of Jesus, the Lamb of God, doesn't simply cover sin, as did the blood of the Jewish sacrifices. His blood takes away sin. There was not a lamb in the entire Old Testament period whose blood could take away sin. "For it is not possible that the blood of bulls and goats could take away sins" (Heb. 10:4).

Those sacrifices were animal sacrifices, and the blood of an animal cannot wash away the sin of a human being who is made in the image of God. Furthermore, those animals weren't voluntary sacrifices; they were taken forcibly to the altar. No lamb ever volunteered to die. But when Jesus Christ came, he was voluntarily the sacrifice for our sin. He willingly gave his life for us (John 10:14–18), and his blood takes away sin and gives complete and final forgiveness. "And their sins and their lawless deeds I will remember no more" (Heb. 8:12).

One Lamb, not many lambs; God's Lamb, not man's lamb; a Lamb whose blood takes away sin, not a lamb whose blood simply covers sin. What a wonderful Savior!

A Lamb for the World's Sin

Notice in John 1:29 that the Lamb of God takes away the sin of *the world*. The circle of God's grace keeps getting larger! First, a ram died for Isaac (see Gen. 22). Then at Passover the Israelites selected a lamb for each household (Exod. 12). In Isaiah 53:7–8, the Lamb died for the nation. So God provided a sacrifice for the individual, for the household, and for the nation. But Jesus Christ was a Lamb sacrificed for *the whole world!*

The gospel of Jesus Christ is the only message that the whole world needs to hear. The gift of eternal life is the only gift the whole world needs to receive and can receive. (If you had to give but one gift to everybody in the world, what would it be?) That's why Christians send out missionaries and support them. If God loves the world and gave his Son to die for the world, how can we keep that message to ourselves?

"This is indeed the Christ, the Savior of the world" (John 4:42). He gives life to the world (John 6:63) and shines as the light of the world (John 8:12). He came to save the world (John 12:47), and therefore it's our responsibility to take the message into all the world (Mark 16:15).

"Worthy Is the Lamb"

The third significant statement concerning Christ the Lamb is found in Revelation 5:12: "Worthy is the Lamb." This chapter records a worship service in heaven. All the choirs of heaven sing the praises of God. "Ten thousand times ten thousand, and thousands of thousands" (v. 11) say with a loud voice, "Worthy is the Lamb" (v. 12). This Lamb, of course, is Jesus Christ.

At least twenty-eight times in the Book of the Revelation, Jesus Christ is referred to as "the Lamb." John didn't use the ordinary word for "lamb"; he used a word meaning "a little pet lamb." The heavenly worshipers praise Jesus and say, "Worthy is the Lamb who was slain to receive power and riches and wisdom, and strength and honor and glory and blessing" (Rev. 5:12).

One day all of God's people will assemble in the courts of heaven and join in that song of praise. "Blessing and honor and glory and power be to Him who sits on the throne, and to the Lamb, forever and ever" (v. 13). "Worthy is the Lamb!" But if we don't worship and praise him on earth today, how can we praise him in heaven? Perhaps the greatest need in the church today is for God's people to return to the sincere worship of God.

"Where is the Lamb?" That is the question of the ages. "Behold! the Lamb of God!" (John 1:29) is the answer to that question. "Worthy is the Lamb" (Rev. 5:12) is our worshipful response to Jesus our Savior. What a delight it is to worship the Lord Jesus and praise him because he died for us.

But, alas, there's a fourth statement that ought to bring tears to the eyes of all of God's people.

"Hide Us from . . . the Lamb!"

The Lamb will one day open the seals in heaven, and judgment will come to the earth. "And the kings of the earth, the great men, the rich men, the commanders, the mighty men, every slave and every free man, hid themselves in the caves and in the rocks of the mountains, and said to the mountains and rocks, 'Fall on us and hide us from the face of Him who sits on the throne and from the wrath of the Lamb! For the great day of His wrath has come, and who is able to stand?'" (Rev. 6:15–17).

What a statement! "Hide us from the . . . wrath of the Lamb!" (v. 16). We rarely associate lambs with wrath. When we think of lambs, we think of weakness and meekness. But the day is coming when those who have rejected Jesus Christ will cry out in fear and try to hide from the face of the Lamb. The Lamb of God will become "the Lion of the tribe of Judah" (Rev. 5:5) and will "roar" at his enemies and judge them.

Everything in the Book of the Revelation relates to the Lamb. The throne is the throne of the Lamb (22:1) and the heavenly city is the temple of the Lamb (21:22). The light in the city is the Lamb: "The Lamb is its light" (21:23). The marriage is the marriage of the Lamb (19:7) and the bride is the wife of the Lamb (21:9). The book that has the names of the saved in it is the Lamb's Book of Life (21:27), and the song that is sung by the victors is the song of Moses and the Lamb (15:3). When we get to heaven, we will not be able to escape the fact that Jesus Christ is God's Lamb!

What a tragedy that many religious people today don't want to hear about Jesus Christ, the Lamb of God. They want Jesus the Teacher, Jesus the Healer, Jesus the Example; but they don't want Jesus the Savior who shed his precious blood to save a sinful world. Some denominations have taken the songs about Christ's blood out of the hymnals, claiming that the idea of blood "offends" unbelievers who attend their services.

What Paul called "the offense of the cross" is still with us, and we must not compromise (1 Cor. 1:18–31). How can you preach the gospel if you leave out the Lamb of God who died on a cross? The gospel says, "Christ died for our sins according to the Scriptures" (1 Cor. 15:3), and if you leave that out, you have no gospel.

"Where is the Lamb?" That question need not be asked anymore because John the Baptist answered it for us when he pointed to Jesus and said, "Behold! the Lamb of God!" (John 1:29). If you have trusted Christ and are living for him, then you're saying in your heart and with your lips, "Worthy is the Lamb" (Rev. 5:12). But if you have not trusted him, one day you will say, "Hide me from the wrath of the Lamb!"

> Guilty, vile and helpless we;
> Spotless Lamb of God was He;
> "Full atonement" can it be?
> Hallelujah! What a Savior!
> (Philip P. Bliss)

127

THE FIRSTBORN

o it was, that while they were there, the days were completed for her to be delivered. And she brought forth her firstborn Son, and wrapped Him in swaddling cloths, and laid Him in a manger, because there was no room for them in the inn" (Luke 2:6–7).

That familiar quotation from Luke's version of the Christmas story reminds us of another name our Lord Jesus Christ wears: "the firstborn." This title is applied to Christ in at least six different verses in the New Testament, so it's worthy of our study.

"Firstborn" was an important word to the Jewish people because the firstborn son in the family inherited many rights and privileges that his siblings didn't enjoy. The firstborn son received the family birthright, the patriarchal blessing, and a double portion of the inheritance (Deut. 21:15–17).

In the Bible, "firstborn" doesn't necessarily mean "born first." Several times in the Old Testament, the Lord gave the rights of the firstborn to somebody else in the family. Ishmael was Abraham's firstborn son, but God gave the inheritance to Isaac; Esau was Isaac's firstborn, but the blessing went to Jacob. When Jacob blessed Joseph's two sons, he reversed the birth order and gave the blessing to Ephraim, the second-born, not to Manasseh, the first-born (Gen. 48). David wasn't Jesse's firstborn, but God made David his firstborn and gave him the throne of Israel (Ps. 89:19–29).

"Firstborn" is a title of position and dignity. The Lord Jesus Christ was indeed Mary's firstborn Son, conceived by the Holy Spirit and born of her virgin womb. According to Mark 6:3, Mary and Joseph had children in the normal course of their marriage, but our Lord was born in a very special way; Joseph was Jesus' foster father, not his biological father. When Mary gave birth to the Lord Jesus, he was literally her firstborn, but later she had children by Joseph.

So the term "firstborn" in the Bible carries with it the idea of dignity and priority. Whoever was firstborn was designated as the very special son in the family. In Exodus 4:22 we read that God designated the people of Israel as his firstborn. So if we think of the word "firstborn" as meaning "priority, superiority, the highest of the high," we will have no problem applying this title to the Lord Jesus Christ.

A careful consideration of the "firstborn" references to Jesus in the New Testament will give us a better understanding of four different aspects of his person and his work:

"He [Christ] is the image of the invisible God, the first-born over all creation" (Col. 1:15).

"And He is the head of the body, the church, who is the beginning, the firstborn from the dead, that in all things He may have the preeminence" (Col. 1:18).

"For whom He foreknew, He also predestined to be conformed to the image of His Son, that He [His Son] might be the firstborn among many brethren" (Rom. 8:29).

"But when He again brings the firstborn into the world, He says, 'Let all the angels of God worship Him'" (Heb. 1:6).

"And from Jesus Christ, the faithful witness, the firstborn from the dead. . . ." (Rev. 1:5).

The Firstborn over All Creation

He is "the firstborn over all creation" (Col. 1:15). The major theme of Colossians is the preeminence of Jesus Christ: "That in all things He [Jesus Christ] may have the preeminence" (Col. 1:18). Paul declares that "Christ is all, and in all" (Col. 3:11).

Christ Is Preeminent

Paul makes it clear that Jesus Christ is preeminent in salvation. "Giving thanks to the Father who has qualified us to be partakers of the inheritance of the saints in the light" (Col. 1:12). "In whom we have redemption through His blood, the forgiveness of sins" (Col. 1:14). Our Lord is preeminent in salvation because he is the only Savior of the world.

He is also preeminent in creation. Colossians 1:16 tells us, "For by Him all things were created." If that's the case, then he himself was not created. Some cultists want us to believe that Jesus Christ was a created being, the highest of the created beings, and therefore not eternal God. But Colossians 1:16 says, "For by him were all things created." Therefore he is not a created thing, for he had to be there before creation in order to create all things.

Note that "all things" includes all things "that are in heaven, and that are on earth, visible and invisible, whether thrones or dominions or principalities or powers. All things were created through Him and for Him. And He is before all things, and in Him all things consist [hold together]"

(Col. 1:16–17). How could anybody read that passage and conclude that Jesus was not eternal God?

Now, if Jesus Christ is preeminent in creation and redemption, should he not be preeminent in our lives and in his church? "And He is the head of the body, the church . . . that in all things He may have the preeminence" (Col. 1:18).

The Highest of All

What does it mean that Jesus is "the firstborn of all creation"? It means that he is the highest of everything in creation. Remember, "firstborn" carries with it the idea of priority, superiority, the highest of the high. The Lord Jesus Christ is superior to everything in creation because he existed prior to creation and he made everything in creation. "All things were made through Him" (John 1:3). "All things were created through Him and for him" (Col. 1:16), and all things are held together by his power. This makes him the highest of the high in all creation.

The Practical Meaning

Why are we having ecological problems today? We have problems with water pollution and air pollution, the wasting of natural resources and the destroying of the beauties and the bounties of nature. Ecological problems are leading to economic problems which, in turn, are leading to political problems.

But why do we have these problems? Primarily, it's because we don't believe in creation anymore. We've taken Christ out of his place of preeminence as the firstborn of all creation, and we're now worshiping and serving the creature instead of the Creator (Rom. 1:25).

We don't see ourselves as stewards of God's gifts in creation; we see ourselves as the masters of the earth. As a result, we have ugliness instead of beauty, destruction instead of growth and development, waste instead of conservation, and greed instead of sharing. We are destroying the very earth God gave us to care for and use for his glory.

People worship the things of creation, the things that they manufacture, instead of the God who gives us these things to enjoy (1 Tim. 6:17). When Jesus Christ is given his proper place as the firstborn of all creation, these problems will be solved. We'll look upon creation as something he has made to be used to glorify and serve him.

We look forward to that day when Jesus will come again and creation will be delivered from bondage and corruption (Rom. 8:18–22). Then we will have a world filled with beauty and harmony, glory and blessing, because the firstborn of all creation, Jesus Christ, will be reigning supremely.

Idolatry

To worship creation rather than the Creator is idolatry, and the Bible condemns idolatry. To become idolaters, we don't have to make ugly idols of wood and stone and fall down to worship them. No, we can make beautiful idols of wood, stone, metal, glass, plastic, and fabric—idols like houses, cars, boats, jewelry, wardrobes, expensive "collectables," furniture, stocks and bonds, and bank accounts. These are the idols that fascinate and control people today and for which they'll sacrifice almost anything.

Does Jesus Christ, the firstborn of all creation, have the preeminence in the way we use the wealth he gives us? Do we see ourselves as stewards of his gracious gifts? Are we faithful to use what he gives us for the good of others and the glory of God? The answers we give to these important questions will help to determine whether or not Jesus is preeminent in our lives.

The Firstborn from the Dead

Jesus Christ is not only the firstborn of all creation, but he is also the firstborn from the dead. He is given this title by Paul in Colossians 1:18 and by the apostle John in Revelation 1:5.

Not the First One Raised

"Firstborn from the dead" doesn't imply that Jesus Christ was the first person ever raised from the dead, because he wasn't. In the Old Testament, at least three people were raised from the dead: the widow's son (1 Kings 17:22), the Shunammite woman's son (2 Kings 4:34–35), and the anonymous man put into Elisha's grave (2 Kings 13:20–21). We have the record of Jesus raising at least three people from the dead (Luke 7:14–15; 8:52–56; and John 11), and it's likely he raised many more (Matt. 11:5).

The title means "the highest and greatest of all who have been raised from the dead." In what ways is Jesus the greatest of all who have been raised from the dead?

He Raised Himself

He is the highest of those who have been raised from the dead because he raised himself by his own power. Our Lord knew he was going to be raised from the dead and he announced it to his disciples (Matt. 16:21; 17:22; 20:17–19). In fact, he raised himself from the dead. "I have power [authority] to lay it [my life] down, and I have power [authority] to take it again" (John 10:18). Lazarus didn't raise himself from the dead, nor did Jairus's daughter or the son of the widow of Nain. But Jesus raised himself from the dead, and this makes him the highest of all who have ever been raised from the dead.

He Can Never Die Again

Not only was he raised from the dead by his own power, but he was raised never to die again. Lazarus died again, Jairus's daughter died again, and so did the son of the widow of Nain. But the Lord Jesus cannot and will not die. He lives "according to the power of an endless life" (Heb. 7:16). Having conquered death, he's now reigning in heaven, and death has no dominion over him. He is the firstborn from among the dead, the highest and the greatest, because he raised himself, never to die again.

He Can and Will Raise Others

He raised himself from the dead and one day he will raise others. We have no record in Scripture that anyone who was raised from the dead ever raised anybody else from the dead. But Jesus will one day return and manifest his resurrection power and authority. He will raise believers to everlasting life, but the unbelieving dead will be raised to face eternal judgment (John 5:24–30; 1 Thess. 4:14–18; Rev. 20:4–6, 11–15).

Christ "has abolished death [rendered it ineffective] and brought life and immortality to light through the gospel" (2 Tim. 1:10). Those who have trusted Christ need not fear death because Jesus is the firstborn from the dead and has conquered death. Death could not hold him (Acts 2:24), and death will not hold us when he calls us to come to be with him.

The Firstborn Among Many Brethren

Romans 8:29 is the third reference to Jesus Christ as the firstborn: "For whom He foreknew, He also predestined to be conformed to the image of His Son, that He [the Son] might be the firstborn among many brethren."

Jesus Christ came and died that he might save sinners and share God's riches with all who will believe in him. It has well been said that God loves his Son so much that he wants everybody else to be just like him. One day you and I will experience the miracle of becoming just like Jesus. "Beloved, now we are children of God; and it has not yet been revealed what we shall be, but we know that when He is revealed, we shall be like Him, for we shall see Him as He is" (1 John 3:2).

Jesus is "bringing many sons to glory" (Heb. 2:10). These are the "many brethren" of Romans 8:29. If Jesus is "the firstborn among many brethren," then his "family" will one day be like him and share his home forever. What he is now, we one day shall be. Jesus is the "last Adam" (1 Cor. 15:45) who died to rescue Adam's sinful race. But he is also "the second Man" (1 Cor. 15:47), because there will be others like him! The church is called "the church of the firstborn" (Heb. 12:23). In one sense, we are the church of the "twice-born." In our first birth, we were unacceptable to God (Eph. 2:1–3), but because of our second birth through faith in Christ, we now have a new nature, the divine nature (2 Peter 1:4). Because we belong to Jesus Christ, we belong to the church of the firstborn, and one day we will share in Christ's glory. He is "the firstborn among many brethren," which assures us that we will be like him. Under the Old Testament Law, the firstborn son inherited twice as much as the others, and he kept it to himself. But Jesus has inherited all things (Heb. 1:2) and he shares his inheritance with all of his brethren!

When will this happen? Hebrews 1:6 gives the answer. The writer is referring to our Lord's coming. "But when He again brings the firstborn into the world, He says, 'Let all the angels of God worship Him.'" Some Bible students believe that this verse refers to Christ's birth at Bethlehem, but I believe the word "again" relates it to the day when

Jesus comes again. When God's firstborn returns, all the angels of God will worship him.

When Jesus came to this planet the first time, the angels worshiped him and sang his praises (Luke 2:8–14). At Bethlehem, he came in humility and weakness; but when he comes again he will come in glory and power. No wonder the angels will sing his praises! When he came the first time, he was a baby in a manger; but when he comes again, he will be the Mighty Conqueror. When he came to Bethlehem it was to accomplish salvation; but when he comes again, it will mean condemnation for his enemies. When he came the first time he wore a crown of thorns; but when he comes again, he will wear a crown of victory.

Jesus Christ is God's firstborn and he will inherit all things and share them with God's family. I trust that you know him as your Savior so that you are sharing in his inheritance today (Eph. 1:3) and looking forward to sharing his glorious inheritance for all eternity.

IMMANUEL

et's consider a title of our Lord Jesus Christ that is used only once in the New Testament and twice in the Old Testament. You'll find the New Testament reference in Matthew 1:23, a quotation from Isaiah 7:14: "'Behold, a virgin shall be with child, and bear a Son, and they shall call His name Immanuel,' which is translated, 'God with us.'" "Immanuel" is also found in Isaiah 8:8.

This prediction takes us back to seven hundred years before the birth of Christ when Ahaz was king of the southern kingdom of Judah (Isa. 7–9). He wasn't a godly man, and at that time he was threatened by a strong coalition of Syria and Israel (the northern kingdom). If Ahaz refused to join with them in opposing Assyria, Rezin and Pekah threatened to attack Judah, depose Ahaz, and put a king of their own choosing on the throne.

But Isaiah the prophet encouraged King Ahaz to trust in the Lord for deliverance and not worry about conspiracies. Ahaz outwardly said that he would, but secretly he had allied himself with Assyria, the enemy Syria and Israel were trying to defeat (2 Kings 16:5–9). It was a cowardly and hypocritical thing to do.

Isaiah encouraged him to trust God because the Lord planned to defeat Israel and Syria (Isa. 7:7–9). Then the prophet encouraged the king to ask God for a sign that would strengthen his faith. In his hypocritical way, Ahaz refused, not because his faith was strong, but because his heart was wicked. The king's confidence wasn't in the Lord; it was in Assyria. If the Lord gave a sign, then Ahaz would have no excuse for his compromising alliance with Assyria.

But God gave a sign anyway, not to Ahaz alone, but to "the house of David" (Isa. 7:13), that is, to the Davidic kings and all the people who were under their authority. The sign was that a woman (who at that time was a virgin) would marry, conceive, and give birth to a son. Before that boy was old enough to discern right from wrong,[1] Syria and Israel would be off the scene. History records that Assyria defeated Syria in 734, and in 722 Assyria conquered Israel and the kingdom came to an end. So much for the enemies of Judah.

Who was this virgin in Isaiah's day that married and gave birth to this "sign son" named Immanuel? We don't know, but some think that Isaiah's first wife had died and he was writing about his second wife. However, this is speculation.[2] But the main thrust in this prophecy is messianic; Isaiah foretold the miraculous conception and virgin birth of Jesus Christ, as recorded in Matthew 1:18–24 and Luke 1:26–38.

Joseph, a just man, was about to divorce Mary to whom he was engaged, because he discovered she was with child. In Jewish society at that time, engagement involved a very strong commitment and was considered as irrevocable as marriage itself. In order to break an engagement, technically you had to go through a divorce. Thinking that Mary had been unfaithful to him, Joseph decided to break their engagement. But an angel spoke to Joseph and told him that Mary wasn't unfaithful but was carrying a child that had been conceived by the Holy Spirit. She would "bring forth a son, and they shall call his name Immanuel." "Immanuel" is a Hebrew word that means "God with us."

Jesus never used this name, nor do we find anyone in the four Gospels calling him by this name. "Immanuel" is really a title, a description of who he is. There are two very wonderful truths that are wrapped up in this title.

Jesus Is God

"'They shall call his name Immanuel,' which being interpreted is, 'God with us'" (Matt. 1:23). There are false teachers who tell us that Jesus Christ is not God, that he was simply a good man or a very godly teacher. Yet from the very beginning of the New Testament, Jesus Christ is called "God." If I called myself "Immanuel" and told you that I was God, you would think I was crazy and rightly so! But Matthew applied to Jesus Christ the title "Immanuel," which means "God with us."

Jesus Claimed to Be God

Jesus Christ claimed to be God, and he did so at the risk of his own life. Jesus said to the Jewish religious leaders, "I and My Father are one." That statement is the next thing to saying, "I am God." What was the result? "Then the Jews took up stones again to stone him." They told him why they intended to stone him: "For a good work we do not stone You, but for blasphemy, and because You, being a Man, make Yourself God" (John 10:31, 33). They understood by his statement "I and My Father are one" that Jesus was claiming to be God, and they were right!

In the upper room, Philip asked Jesus, "Lord, show us the Father, and it is sufficient for us." Jesus replied to him, "Have I been with you so long, and yet you have not known Me, Philip? He who has seen Me has seen the Father" (John 14:8–9). Once again Jesus claimed to be God. To see Jesus is to see God.

The Jews told Pilate, "We have a law, and according to our law He ought to die, because He made Himself the Son of God" (John 19:7). The Jewish religious leaders had no problem understanding what Jesus was talking about. They knew that Jesus was claiming to be God, and to them that was the height of blasphemy.

Jesus Received Worship As God

More than claiming to be God, Jesus received worship as God. To worship any creature is idolatry because it's commanded: "You shalt worship the LORD your God, and Him only you shall serve" (Matt. 4:10, quoted from Deut. 6:13). When Jesus was but a little child, the Magi came and worshiped him (Matt. 2:11). When Jesus walked on the water and then calmed the great storm, the disciples in the ship worshiped him (Matt. 14:22–33). The man born blind whom Jesus healed worshiped him (John 9:38).

Jesus accepted worship! This means that he was God and he knew he was God. This worship was perfectly proper and he received it. Either Jesus is what he claimed to be and therefore deserves our worship, or he is a deceiver or perhaps a madman; but all the evidence points to the fact that Jesus Christ is Immanuel, "God with us."

Jesus Is Called God

A number of times in the New Testament, Jesus is specifically called God. Let's note some of these references.

John 1:1 says, "In the beginning was the Word, and the Word was with God, and the Word was God." The title "Word" refers to Jesus Christ, because John 1:14 says, "And the Word became flesh and dwelt among us," a reference to the incarnation of our Lord.

In John 1:18, Jesus Christ is called God. The King James Version says, "No man hath seen God at any time; the only begotten Son, which is in the bosom of the Father, he hath declared [unfolded, explained] him." The only way Jesus could do this was to be God himself. The New International Version translates this verse, "God the One and Only, who is at the Father's side, has made him known." The New American Standard Bible translates it, "The only begotten God, who is in the bosom of the Father, He has explained Him." The combined thrust of these translations is that Jesus is God.

In Romans 9:5, the apostle Paul describes the blessings God gave to the nation of Israel, and he writes: "Of whom are the fathers and from whom, according to the flesh, Christ came, who is over all, the eternally blessed God. Amen." Titus 2:13 is very clear: "Looking for the blessed hope and glorious appearing of our great God and Savior Jesus Christ." Our Savior is God! In Hebrews 1:8 we read that God the Father said to God the Son, "Your throne, O God, is forever and ever."

Second Peter 1:1 reads: "Simon Peter, a bondservant and apostle of Jesus Christ, To those who have obtained like precious faith with us by the righteousness of God and Savior Jesus Christ." One Person, two titles: "God and our Savior Jesus Christ."

First John 5:20 clinches the argument: "And we know that the Son of God has come and has given us an understanding, that we may know Him who is true, and we are in Him who is true, in His Son Jesus Christ. This is the true God and eternal life." The Lord Jesus Christ is God!

Jesus Is God with Us

There is a second truth that comes from the name "Immanuel." Not only is Jesus Christ eternal God, but he is God with us. He isn't a God who is far away, distant, and unconcerned; he's with us where we are, sharing the experiences of our lives. When Jesus Christ was born of the Virgin Mary and came into this world as a little baby, he identified with all aspects of humanity. He is the God-man; he is God, and he is God with us.

Frequently in Scripture you find the wonderful promise, "I am with you." God gave that promise to Moses (Exod. 33:14) and he gave it to Joshua, Moses' successor. He said, "As I was with Moses, so I will be with you" (Josh. 1:5; see Deut. 31:6–8). The Lord has given that same promise to us. Matthew began his Gospel by introducing "God with us" (1:23), and he ended his book on the same note: "Lo, I am with you always, even to the end of the age" (Matt. 28:20). The Lord Jesus Christ is "God with us" in every area of life.

In Salvation

He is with us in salvation. He is a holy God, and he ought to be against us and far from us because we're an unholy people. But he is with us in salvation. If you will open your heart to him, he will come in, and he will be with you forever. He will forgive you; he will fellowship with you; he will guide you and fulfill his purposes in your life.

In Our Trials

Jesus is with us in the trials of life. How many times I have turned to Isaiah 43:2, and I have read this promise for my own benefit and for the encouragement of others:

"When you pass through the waters, I will be with you; and through the rivers, they shall not overflow you. When you walk through the fire, you shall not be burned, nor shall the flame scorch you." Isaiah 43:5 says, "Fear not: for I am with you. . . ."

In Isaiah 41:10, we read: "Fear not, for I am with you; be not dismayed, for I am your God. I will strengthen you, yes, I will help you; I will uphold you with My righteous right hand." No matter what the circumstances Jesus Christ is with us to guard us and help us succeed.

These promises in Isaiah remind me of the experience of Daniel's three friends who defied the orders of King Nebuchadnezzar and refused to bow before his golden image (Dan. 3). The king had the three men thrown bound into the fiery furnace; but when he investigated, he was astonished at what he saw. Not only were the three Jewish men free from their bonds and walking unhurt in the furnace, but there was a fourth man with them! "The form of the fourth," said the king, "is like the Son of God!" (Dan. 3:25). When these men of faith went through the fire, Jesus was there with them. He is Immanuel, "God with us."

In Our Service

Jesus Christ is with us in our service, as we seek to please him and do his will. "And they went out and preached everywhere, the Lord working with them. . . ." (Mark 16:20). Not only is he walking with us, but he is also working with us. We shouldn't get weary of the Lord's work because serving God is exciting, and we are thrilled with the privilege he gives us to serve him. It is good to know that the Lord is working with us and we aren't alone.

When Paul was seeking to found a church in Corinth (Acts 18), he was confronted with severe opposition, as is often the case when we invade the enemy's territory. Then

143

the Lord appeared to Paul and said, "Do not be afraid, but speak, and do not keep silent; for I am with you. . . ." (Acts 18:9).

The Lord stood with Paul to the very end of his ministry, even though many of his friends forsook him. When a prisoner in Rome, Paul wrote, "At my first defense no one stood with me, but all forsook me. May it not be charged against them. But the Lord stood with me and strengthened me. . . ." (2 Tim. 4:16–17). Jesus is Immanuel, "God with us."

In Our Sorrows

Christ is with us in the sorrows of life, as we go through bereavement and the painful separation that accompanies the death of somebody we love. The promise is in Psalm 23:4: "Yea, though I walk through the valley of the shadow of death, I will fear no evil; for You art with me. . . ." Jesus is with us in the sorrows of life and gives us the strength and comfort we need.

Death is an enemy because it robs us of those we love and leaves us with hearts that are empty and lonely. Some people try to heal their broken hearts by turning to drink or narcotics or a busy schedule of entertainment and travel, but this approach only distracts us temporarily from reality and postpones the pain. When Jesus comes to us in the valley, he helps us to accept the facts of life and death, face them honestly, and deal with them believingly. Charles Wesley wrote in his hymn "Jesus, Lover of My Soul":

> Other refuge have I none;
> Hangs my helpless soul on Thee;
> Leave, ah! leave me not alone,
> Still support and comfort me.
> All my trust on Thee is stayed,

All my help from Thee I bring;
Cover my defenseless head
With the shadow of Thy wing.

But even in our own death, Jesus will be with us. In my
pastoral ministry, many times I've helped families lay their
loved ones to rest. Often a family member will grieve exces-
sively because the loved one died alone. *No child of God ever
dies alone!* According to 1 Thessalonians 4:14, our Christian dead "sleep in Jesus," which literally means "are put to
sleep through Jesus." In his Expanded Translation of the
New Testament, the Greek scholar Dr. Kenneth Wuest
translates this verse "God will bring with Him those who
have fallen asleep through the intermediate agency of Jesus."
Jesus is there at the hour of death to put to sleep the bodies of his beloved and to take their spirits to heaven. No
child of God ever dies alone.

With Us Forever!

Jesus will be with us throughout all eternity! When the
apostle John saw that Holy City coming down from heaven,
he heard a great voice saying, "Behold, the tabernacle of
God is with men, and He will dwell with them, and they
shall be His people. God Himself will be with them and be
their God" (Rev. 21:3). "They shall see His face . . . and
there shall be no night there" (Rev. 22:4–5). Even in heaven,
Jesus will be "Immanuel . . . God with us."

But those who reject Jesus Christ won't spend eternity
in his glorious and loving presence. "They will be punished
with everlasting destruction and shut out from the presence of the Lord and from the majesty of his power"
(2 Thess. 1:9 NIV). Instead of enjoying "God with us," the
unsaved will experience "God apart from us" as they spend
eternity separated from God.

145

Not only for this life, but even more for the life hereafter, it's wise to trust Jesus Christ and walk with him. He is Immanuel, "God with us"; he will be with you in every circumstance of life. Will you trust him?

Jesus Christ is God; trust him, worship him, give your very best to him. And Jesus Christ is God with us. Wherever we are, in the difficulties and demands of life, Jesus Christ is right there.

"Immanuel . . . God with us." Are you trusting him today? Have you surrendered your all to him? This is what he wants us to do, for he is God with us.

JESUS

The name you give to your child may not determine his or her destiny, but the name that was given to our Lord was a part of his destiny. "Then the angel said to her, 'Do not be afraid, Mary, for you have found favor with God. And behold, you will conceive in your womb and bring forth a Son, and shall call His name JESUS'" (Luke 1:30–31). "You shall call His name JESUS, for He will save His people from their sins" (Matt. 1:21).

In our modern society, there are two names that very few people would give to their sons. One is "Judas" because that name is too terrible; the other is "Jesus" because that name is too wonderful.

We come now to that wonderful name which means the most to all of God's people, the name "Jesus."

> How sweet the name of Jesus sounds
> In a believer's ear!
> It soothes his sorrows, heals his wounds.
> And drives away his fear.
> Dear name! The Rock on which I build,

147

My Shield and Hiding-place,
My never-failing Treas'ry, filled
With boundless stores of grace.

(John Newton)

Sometimes the name "Jesus" is used in blasphemy. Sometimes it's sung or spoken rather carelessly and casually. Yet "Jesus" is a very special name. Let me share four facts with you that help us to better understand the wonder of the name "Jesus."

A Name Given from Heaven

The name "Jesus" was a name given from heaven, commanded by the angel before Mary had conceived the baby in her womb. Whenever a child is born, the parents have to answer the question: "What shall we call the baby?" I have some friends who waited five or six days before naming their last child, and the hospital was somewhat perturbed about this. With the Lord Jesus, there was no problem because the name was given from heaven.

First, the angel gave the name to the mother, Mary (Luke 1:31): "And behold, you will conceive in your womb and bring forth a Son, and shall call His name JESUS." Mary believed God's promise and yielded herself fully to the Spirit to accomplish the will of God. "Behold the maidservant of the Lord! Let it be to me according to your word" (Luke 1:38).

Then the name was given to Joseph, the foster father of Jesus. Joseph had considered putting Mary away because he thought she had sinned, but God said to him, "Joseph, son of David, do not be afraid to take to you Mary your wife, for that which is conceived in her is of the Holy Spirit. And she will bring forth a Son, and you shall call His name JESUS, for He will save His people from their sins" (Matt. 1:20–21).

148

Occasionally in Bible history, special babies were given their names directly by the Lord. Hagar's son by Abraham was named "Ishmael" (Gen. 16:11), and Abraham and Sarah's son "Isaac" was also named by God before the baby was born (Gen. 17:19). God commanded Zechariah and Elizabeth to call their son "John" (Luke 1:13), and we know him as "John the Baptist."

But it's only reasonable that the Son of God should be named by his Father in heaven because the Lord Jesus Christ came from heaven. He wasn't begotten by Joseph; he was conceived in Mary's womb by the Holy Spirit. He was sent from heaven!

Frequently in the Gospel of John, Jesus spoke about coming down from heaven and being sent by the Father. Every baby born into this world is a person who has never existed before. But when Jesus came into this world, he had existed from all eternity, so his birth had to be different. He came from heaven, sent by the Father; therefore, his name was given from heaven.

He came to do a work that only heaven could do: save people from their sins. "For God so loved the world that He gave His only begotten Son, that whoever believes in Him should not perish but have everlasting life. For God did not send His Son into the world to condemn the world, but that the world through Him might be saved" (John 3:16–17). Salvation is of the Lord because nobody can save himself.

His name was given from heaven because one day he is going to take his people to heaven. "I go to prepare a place for you. And if I go and prepare a place for you, I will come again and receive you to Myself; that where I am, there you may be also" (John 14:2–3). The name of Jesus was a name given from heaven.

A Name Great in History

The name of Jesus is a name great in history. "Jesus" is the Greek form of "Joshua," or "Jehoshua," which means "Jehovah is salvation." This name belonged to two famous men in Jewish history.

Joshua the Conqueror

Joshua was the man who assisted Moses (Exod. 24:13; Num. 11:28) and then became Moses' successor (Num. 27:18–20). Joshua led the people into the Promised Land where they claimed their inheritance and defeated their enemies. In Numbers 13:8 we have his name given as "Oshea," or "Hoshea," which means "salvation." But Moses changed his name from "Hoshea" to "Jehoshua," which means "Jehovah is salvation" (Num. 13:16).

Throughout history, the Jewish people have delighted in giving their sons the name "Joshua," because it's the name of a hero; it means "Jehovah is salvation." Not only does the name look back to a great past, but it also reminds them of a great future, when Jehovah will redeem his people Israel and establish them in their kingdom.

But the name "Joshua" has even greater significance. According to Hebrews 4:8, Joshua points to our Lord Jesus Christ. To begin with, Joshua followed Moses, and Joshua, not Moses, led the people into their inheritance. Moses represents the Law, but Joshua represents the victory that comes by grace. "For the law was given through Moses, but grace and truth came through Jesus Christ" (John 1:17). Moses wanted to enter the Promised Land, but God wouldn't let him because it was ordained that Joshua lead the people into Canaan and conquer the enemy.

The Law can't give you your inheritance. It isn't possible by the keeping of the Law to enter into the inheritance that God has for you in this life, the "rest" that you can have through faith in Jesus Christ. Joshua, not Moses, led the people into their rest (Heb. 3:1–4:16). It is Jesus who gives us rest. He is our Joshua, for he has conquered all our enemies, including the last enemy, death (1 Cor. 15:26). When you know Jesus as your Savior, then you have entered into your "salvation inheritance" and you have "all spiritual blessings" through him (Eph. 1:3).

But every child of God has a special inheritance assigned by the Lord that involves using our gifts and resources to serve the Lord and his people and to win the lost. "Eye has not seen, nor ear heard, nor have entered into the heart of man the things which God has prepared for those who love Him. But God has revealed them to us through His Spirit" (1 Cor. 2:9–10). We often apply this passage to heaven, but I believe Paul was writing about our lives on earth here and now. "For we are His workmanship, created in Christ Jesus for good works, which God prepared beforehand that we should walk in them" (Eph. 2:10).

When you read the Book of Joshua, you discover that God had the plans all worked out for his people. All Joshua had to do was get his orders from the Lord and obey them by faith, and the victory was won. On two occasions (Josh. 7–10), Joshua ran ahead of the Lord and failed to wait for orders, and that's when he tasted shameful defeat. But as long as Joshua took his orders from the Lord and obeyed them, the people of Israel conquered the enemy and claimed their inheritance.

Jesus Christ is our Joshua, our Jehoshua—"Jehovah is salvation." What the Lord told Joshua in Joshua 1 certainly applies to us today. We must feed on the Word of God, meditate on it, and obey it. "Not one thing has failed of all the good things which the LORD your God spoke concerning you," Joshua reminded the people before he died. "All have come to pass for you, and not one word of them has failed" (Josh. 23:14). We can rest on God's promises because he never fails.

Joshua the High Priest

The second famous person in the Old Testament who had this name was Joshua the high priest (Ezra 2:2; 3:2, 8; 5:2; Hag. 1:1; 2:2; Zech. 3; 6:9–15). Joshua was the high priest when the remnant of Jews left Babylon and returned to the land to rebuild the temple. Zerubbabel was the governor of the nation, and the prophets were Haggai and Zechariah.

The prophet Zechariah did something to Joshua the high priest that had never been done to any high priest in Jewish history: he put a crown on his head (Zech. 6:9–15)! Under the Mosaic law, priests were not to be kings and kings were not to be priests. King Uzziah tried to be a priest and God smote him with leprosy (2 Chron. 26:16–21).

But Joshua the high priest is a picture of our Lord Jesus Christ who is both king and priest. One of the basic themes of the Book of Hebrews is that Jesus isn't a high priest like Aaron, but like Melchizedek, who was a king and a priest (Gen. 14:18–24; Heb. 5:10; 6:20; chaps. 7–9).

Melchizedek is mentioned in only two places in the Old Testament: Genesis 14:18–24 and Psalm 110:4. There is no record in the Bible of his ancestry or his death, and in this way is a picture of Jesus Christ, our heavenly King-Priest. The priests who descended from Aaron were never kings, and when they died they had to be replaced. But Christ's priesthood doesn't come from Aaron; it comes from Melchizedek. Therefore, he is both King and Priest and his priesthood will never end.

Joshua the general and Joshua the high priest were two great men in Jewish history. They remind us that the name "Jesus" is a name great in history.

A Name Glorious in Honor

Fact number three: "Jesus" is a name glorious in honor. It is interesting that even though the name "Jesus" (the Greek form of "Joshua") was a common name among the Jews in the first century, it stopped being used after the second century. The people of Israel, scattered abroad after the fall of Jerusalem in 70 A.D., didn't want to be identified with that name. Was it because Jesus Christ had been given that name and the Jews thought he had desecrated it? Jesus was known as "Jesus of Nazareth" to distinguish him from all the other men who were named "Jesus" (or "Joshua") in that day.

Pilate wrote an inscription and put it on the cross: "THIS IS JESUS OF NAZARETH, THE KING OF THE JEWS." Imagine the Jewish people seeing the great name "Joshua" nailed to a cross! But our Lord took that name and lifted it to the highest heavens: "Therefore God also has highly exalted Him and given Him the name which is above every name, that at the name of Jesus every knee should bow, of those in heaven, and of those on earth, and of those under the earth, and that every tongue should confess that Jesus Christ is Lord, to the glory of God the Father" (Phil. 2:9–11).

Jesus is indeed a name glorious in honor. Do you know why? Because Jesus Christ meets our greatest need, which is salvation from sin and victory over sin. He alone can meet that need. To do this, he paid the greatest price: he died on the cross, arose, and went back to heaven where he now intercedes for us. He secured for us the greatest gifts, gifts that will last forever. Yes, the name of Jesus is a name given from heaven, a name great in history, a name glorious in honor.

A Name Gracious in Help

Fact number four: It is a name gracious in help. Wherever people heard the name "Jesus," they knew what it meant: "Jehovah is salvation." Jesus came "to seek and to save that which was lost" (Luke 19:10).

In Mark 10:46–52, blind Bartimaeus was sitting by the roadside begging. He heard a crowd going by, and his ears told him there was something different about the crowd. He asked, "What's happening? Who is going by?" The people replied, "Jesus of Nazareth is passing by." In other words, "salvation" was passing by! Encouraged by that name, Bartimaeus cried out and said, "Jesus, Son of David, have mercy on me!" (Mark 10:47). The people tried to silence the beggar, but he persisted all the more: "Son of David, have mercy on me!" Our Lord stopped and called the man, and he went to Jesus who cured him and saved him. The name of Jesus is gracious in help for all who call upon him.

The thief on the cross saw the sign above the head of Jesus: "THIS IS JESUS OF NAZARETH, THE KING OF THE JEWS." (Matt. 27:37). That name "Jesus" gave him hope and the thief trusted Jesus and was given entrance into paradise.

The Lord Jesus is gracious in his help. Through the name of Jesus we can have salvation. Through the name of Jesus we pray. In the name of Jesus Christ we are able to conquer the evil one. Nobody else can do what Jesus can do, for "there is no other name under heaven given among men by which we must be saved" (Acts 4:12).

The religious leaders in Jerusalem tried to get the apostles to stop preaching and teaching in the name of Jesus, but they failed (Acts 4:1–22). Peter and John had healed a lame man in the name of Jesus (Acts 3:6), and this led to the salvation of at least two thousand people (Acts 2:41; 4:4). This event angered the religious leaders who wanted the people to believe that Jesus was dead. So they threatened Peter and John and tried to silence them. But Peter told them, "We cannot but speak the things which we have seen and heard" (Acts 4:20).

Great names come and go, but the name of Jesus remains. The devil still hates it, the world still opposes it, but God still blesses it and we can still claim it! "In the name of Jesus" is the key that unlocks the door of prayer and the treasury of God's grace. It's the weapon that defeats the enemy and the motivation that compels our sacrifice and service. It's the name that causes our hearts to rejoice and our lips to sing his praise.

"That at the name of Jesus every knee should bow . . . and that every tongue should confess that Jesus Christ is Lord, to the glory of God the Father" (Phil. 2:10–11).

"Hallowed be Your name" (Matt. 6:9).

POSTSCRIPT

What is your name?

We have thought about some of the names of the Lord Jesus Christ. The next question is: What is your name?

God asked that question of Jacob as he wrestled with him that midnight hour. "And Jacob was left alone; and there wrestled a man with him until the breaking of the day. And he [the Lord] said unto him, What is thy name? And He said, Jacob" (Gen. 32:24, 27). The name "Jacob" means "supplanter" and carries with it the idea of scheming and lying to get what you want. The first step toward appropriating all that Christ has for you is admitting to him what you really are. What is your name?

Is it liar, fighter, rebel, pretender, fearful, hateful?

What is your name? Admit it to the Lord right now, and let him agree with you. You gain nothing by pretending. Then ask him to forgive you for what you are, and tell him to make you what you ought to be in Christ. Claim for yourself by faith all that Christ is and all that he does.

All of us occasionally assume roles in order to get out of life what we think we ought to have. Life is dull, so we assume the role of spectator or entertainer in order to get some enjoyment. What we really need is Jesus Christ, for his name is Wonderful, and that takes care of the dullness of life.

Life is complicated, and we have to make decisions, so we assume some role in order to try to make some sense out of life. What we really need is Jesus Christ, for his name is Counselor, and that take care of the decisions of life.

Life is demanding. Some people assume the role of a tyrant in order to succeed in this demanding world; others give up and become slaves or tools or even invalids. But what we need is Jesus Christ, for his name is the Mighty God, and that takes care of the demands of life.

Life becomes narrow and limited. We feel like we are packed in a coffin. Perhaps we rebel and try to enlarge our sphere of experience. Perhaps we give up the battle and crawl about in our tiny world, creeping like ants when we should be flying like eagles. What we need is Jesus Christ, for his name is the Everlasting Father, the Father of Eternity, and this takes care of the dimensions of life.

Life is full of disturbances. Without are fightings, within are fears. There is no peace. A dozen open doors beckon us to some kind of peace—escape, entertainment, alcohol, sex, dope, over-work—we run from one substitute to another hoping to find peace. What we need is Jesus Christ, for his name is Prince of Peace, and that takes care of the disturbances of life. "Thou wilt keep him in perfect peace, whose mind is stayed on thee, because he trustest in thee" (Isa. 26:3 KJV).

What is your name? Jacob admitted his name—and shame—to the Lord, and the Lord changed his name! God said to Jacob, "Your name shall no longer be called Jacob, but Israel; for you have struggled with God and with men, and have prevailed" (Gen. 32:28).

157

God can change your name. "Thou art Simon," said Jesus to Andrew's brother. "Thou shalt be called Cephas," which means "a stone" (John 1:42 KJV).

Tell God what you are. Believe what he is. Yield yourself to him.

Put the government of your life upon his shoulder.

When you do, you'll discover who he is: Wonderful, Counselor, the Mighty God, the Everlasting Father, the Prince of Peace.

And what he is, you will share!

Is the government of your life on his shoulder?

NOTES

Chapter 4: The Everlasting Father

1. Henry F. Lyte, "Abide With Me," verse 2.

Chapter 6: The Nazarene

1. Actually both Jonah and Nahum came from towns in Galilee, Jonah from Gath-hepher in Zebulun (2 Kings 14:25), and Nahum from Elkosh (Nahum 1:1), which has traditionally been placed in Galilee.

2. A different Hebrew word (*tzehmah*) is used for the "Branch" messianic prophecies in Isaiah 4:2; Jeremiah 23:5 and 33:15; and Zechariah 3:8 and 6:12. D. A. Carson writes, "It is possible at the same time that there is a discreet allusion to the *netser* (branch) of Isaiah 11:1. . ." (*Expositor's Bible Commentary,* Frank E. Gaebelein, editor; vol. 8, p. 97). But Matthew wrote of *fulfillment* and that suggests specific prophecies.

3. *Metropolitan Tabernacle Pulpit,* vol. 27, p. 672.

Chapter 7: The Pioneer

1. When Jesus compared faith to a "grain of mustard seed," the smallest seed people knew at that time (Matt. 17:20), he was speaking of the dynamic life within the seed and not the smallness of the seed. Living faith in a living God is a dynamic force that must grow and express itself. "Mustard Seed" faith is faith that is vital and dynamic.

Chapter 12: The Firstborn

1. This law explains Elisha's request that Elijah give him a double portion of his spirit (2 Kings 2:1–15). He was asking to be treated like Elijah's firstborn son, but he wanted a spiritual inheritance, not a material one.

2. Often God rearranged the birth order and chose the younger rather than the elder. Ishmael was Abraham's firstborn son, but God chose Isaac; Esau was Isaac's firstborn, but God gave the inheritance to Jacob. When Jacob blessed Joseph's two sons, he put Ephraim, the younger, ahead of Manasseh (Gen. 48).

The other two references are Hebrews 11:28 (the firstborn in Egypt) and Hebrews 12:23 ("the church of the firstborn").

3. During his earthly ministry, Christ's half-brothers did not believe in him (John 7:1–9; Ps. 69:8; Matt. 12:46–50); but after his resurrection, they did become believers and a part of the fellowship (Acts 1:14).

4. The Levites were dedicated to God in the place of the firstborn to serve him and assist the priests (Num. 3:11–13, 45).

5. "Those who have done good" and "those who have done evil" are phrases that describe the saved and the lost. Paul uses similar wording in Romans 2:5–11. There's no suggestion here that sinners can be saved by their good works.

6. Predestination in Scripture describes God's wise plan to accomplish certain things for his own people. They are predestined to be like Jesus Christ (Rom. 8:29), which Ephesians 1:5 calls "the adoption" and Romans 8:18–23 says will occur when Jesus returns. We are also predestined to share God's glorious inheritance (Eph. 1:5; 1 Peter 1:3–4).

Chapter 13: Immanuel

1. Some interpreters take this to mean "before he becomes a son of the Law at age twelve."

2. The fact that Isaiah's first two sons were "signs" to the nation may argue that the mother was the prophet's wife (Isa. 7:3; 8:1–4). Some students see a parallel between Isa. 7:14–17 and 8:1–4. However, the birth in Isaiah's day was not a virgin birth. The woman was a virgin when the prophecy was given, but the son was conceived in a natural way.

Warren W. Wiersbe is Distinguished Professor of Preaching at Grand Rapids Baptist Seminary and has pastored churches in Indiana, Kentucky, and Illinois (Chicago's historic Moody Church). He is the author of more than 100 books, including *God Isn't in a Hurry*, *The Bumps Are What You Climb On*, and *The Bible Exposition Commentary* (2 vols.).